KILL 'EM ALL

INTRODUCTION

The history of heavy metal music has been marked by a series of quantum jumps. Consider this simplified yet revealing natural progression:

Cream, Jimi Hendrix, Yardbirds	mid 60's
Led Zeppelin, Deep Purple, Black Sabbath	late 60's/early 70's
AC/DC, Judas Priest, Scorpions	mid 70's
Motorhead, Iron Maiden, Tygers of Pan Tang	late 70's
Van Halen, Randy Rhoads, Dio	early 80's

Representing the next evolutionary epoch in the artform, the dynamic new approach—marketed under the various categories of speed metal, thrash, hardcore, etc.—leapt upon an unsuspecting but appreciative heavy metal audience in the mid 1980's. As the nature of the music gets heavier, the change just seems inevitable. John Sykes (currently of Blue Murder, formerly of Whitesnake and originally the blazing lead guitarist of Tygers of Pan Tang—a seminal influence cited by James Hetfield) had this to say on the subject in a conversation we had in mid 1989: "In Tygers, we were taking the speed and heaviness a step further than Purple, Zeppelin or Sabbath... they called it 'The New Wave of British Heavy Metal' [NWOBHM]. But it's energy—no matter what, it always seems to get the kids going. Now we've got bands like Metallica, who are still faster and heavier, and it's good. It's good that the music is evolving."

Taking its inspiration from this NWOBHM, thrash had more or less provided an alternative to the insipid poseur trappings of the glam scene, the Van Halen clone phenomenon pouring out of L.A. and the dungeonistic leather 'n' chains format of mainstream metal. It was fresh, irrepressible and thought provoking—musically, lyrically, conceptually. Distinguished by excessive speed (up-tempo grooves precisely executed), intensity and complexity in riffs and rhythm figures, ambitious arrangements and intricate formal structures fraught with multiple tempos, unusual modulations, meter changes and tonal ambiguity, precarious balances of sophistication and rawness in guitar soloing and socially conscious lyrics and imagery, one senses an overall conviction in both physical performance and artistic philosophy. Since thrash's inception, a handful of important groups have come to define and embody the new music: Anthrax, Exodus, Megadeth, Testament, M.O.D. and, of course, Metallica.

When Metallica released their debut album *Kill 'Em All* in 1984, they were emerging as a vital new voice in the underground Bay Area thrash movement. Guitarist/composer/vocalist James Hetfield and drummer/composer Lars Ulrich had moved up to the San Francisco vicinity to escape the confines of a dreary L.A. rock scene, comprised largely of Ratt's, Motley Crüe's and related spinoffs. There, they hooked up with bassist Cliff Burton and finally replaced guitarist Dave Mustaine (now with Megadeth) with the multi-faceted Kirk Hammett, just prior to the tracking of *Kill 'Em All*. The rest is history. Metallica has attained near-legendary status as the leading speed metal band of the 1980's—the fact reinforced by numerous sold-out concert appearances, a more than successful recording career and the unprecedented exposure in the genre (MTV, etc.).

All the signature devices which make Metallica's music so striking and immediately recognizable are well-displayed on *Kill 'Em All*. Their riffs are beyond heavy, delivered with a thick, distorted sound and the unmistakable downstroke attack of Hetfield and Hammett. Prime examples can be heard in the rhythm figures to practically any song on the record, with "The Four Horsemen" being particularly noteworthy. Compare the variety of approaches utilized: heavy palm muting of a simple but effective three-note riff against an E pedal (6th string open) in Rhy. Fig. 1, a muted, triplet E pedal "gallop" motif under power chords E5, D, C5 and G5 in Rhy. Fig. 2, sustaining power chords E5, D5, C5 and B5 in Rhy. Fig. 3, and the unusual E Phrygian mode alluded to in Rhy. Figs. 4 and 5. Rhy. Fig. 4 states this in no uncertain terms with a characteristic F5 to E5

chord move, and Rhy. Fig. 5 incorporates a C5—>C#5—>D5 chromatic progression into the E minor sound. The familiar tritone dissonance is present in the repertoire as expected. Check out the riffs in "Jump in the Fire" (Rhy. Fig. 2—tritone of Db against G), "Whiplash" (chorus: Rhy. Fig. 3—F# against C), "Metal Militia" (Rhy. Fig. 1—Bb against E and Rhy. Figs. 2 and 3—Eb5 against an A minor tonal center) and the intro to "Am I Evil?" where the E—>Bb relationship is presented in a number of ways: chordally in bars 5-7, and in single-note form in bars 13 and 14—foreshadowing its prominent harmonic role in the chorus.

Tempo changes? Naturally. The examples are plentiful. In "The Four Horsemen," a fast rock shuffle at ♩=204 changes to half time (Riff B) ♩=102 and then abruptly gives way to a faster straight-eighth feel at ♩=164. The latter two tempo changes are further complicated by a meter change of 4/4 to 2/4 to 4/4. Metallica handles them with an ease that is virtually telepathic. Consider also the various tempo fluctuations in "Am I Evil?" The intro begun moderately at ♩=100 proceeds to free time (one bar, conducted by feel) and then to a blistering speed of ♩=240. The verse, pre-chorus and chorus are at ♩=160, with Rhy. Fig. 4 picking up momentum to a faster triplet feel to ♩=192 for the bridge and guitar solo.

Feel changes and meter changes occur with such regularity that they must be perceived as idiomatic. Note the interesting use of three bars of 4/4 and one of 7/8 as a consistent rhythmic sequence in the chorus and solo of "Hit the Lights" (see the composite figure of Rhy. Fig. 3 plus Riff B in the solo). Other examples can be found in "Whiplash" (intro and solo), "Motorbreath" (going into Guitar solo I with a 5/4 bar and into Guitar solo II with a 2/4 bar) and within "Blitzkrieg" (Rhy. Fig. 1). "Phantom Lord" provides a clear-cut sample of the band's ability to change feel in the interlude between guitar solos, but the album as a whole is absolutely teeming with countless other similar events skillfully arranged and precisely executed in trademark Metallica fashion. It would be an invaluable experience to track them down for yourself. Start with "Whiplash," "No Remorse" and "The Four Horsemen."

Kirk Hammett's distinctive solos grace *Kill 'Em All* from one end to the other. His style is the fusion of a blues-based hard rock attitude a la Schenker, Aerosmith, Hendrix and Beck, with classically-tinged Euro-metal shadings (in the vein of Uli Roth and Randy Rhoads) and a fair portion of abstract modernism (no doubt fostered by close contact with teacher Joe Satriani). His well-known solos run the gamut from fast staccato and muted picked runs and legato scale lines to relentless repeating riffs (frequently involving open-string pull-offs), bluesy, emotional string bending and finger vibrato, and the mandatory 80's guitar mannerisms (two-handed tap-ons, neat noises and whammy bar tricks). Definitive solos occur in "Whiplash," "Seek and Destroy" and "Hit the Lights" (these feature some "outside" extended chromatic licks), "Phantom Lord" and "Motorbreath" (played with his familiar wah wah pedal tone) and "The Four Horsemen" with its quirky cross-relation dissonance of C-natural and C-sharp (note to chord relationship) in Guitar solo I. At this point in Kirk's career, he was based largely in the pentatonic and blues tonalities with brief, contrasting episodes of modality, chromaticism and ostinato incorporated into his soloing as thematic and melodic tangents.

- Wolf Marshall

4

KILL 'EM ALL

INTRODUCTION

The history of heavy metal music has been marked by a series of quantum jumps. Consider this simplified yet revealing natural progression:

Cream, Jimi Hendrix, Yardbirds	mid 60's
Led Zeppelin, Deep Purple, Black Sabbath	late 60's/early 70's
AC/DC, Judas Priest, Scorpions	mid 70's
Motorhead, Iron Maiden, Tygers of Pan Tang	late 70's
Van Halen, Randy Rhoads, Dio	early 80's

Representing the next evolutionary epoch in the artform, the dynamic new approach—marketed under the various categories of speed metal, thrash, hardcore, etc.—leapt upon an unsuspecting but appreciative heavy metal audience in the mid 1980's. As the nature of the music gets heavier, the change just seems inevitable. John Sykes (currently of Blue Murder, formerly of Whitesnake and originally the blazing lead guitarist of Tygers of Pan Tang—a seminal influence cited by James Hetfield) had this to say on the subject in a conversation we had in mid 1989: "In Tygers, we were taking the speed and heaviness a step further than Purple, Zeppelin or Sabbath... they called it 'The New Wave of British Heavy Metal' [NWOBHM]. But it's energy—no matter what, it always seems to get the kids going. Now we've got bands like Metallica, who are still faster and heavier, and it's good. It's good that the music is evolving."

Taking its inspiration from this NWOBHM, thrash had more or less provided an alternative to the insipid poseur trappings of the glam scene, the Van Halen clone phenomenon pouring out of L.A. and the dungeonistic leather 'n' chains format of mainstream metal. It was fresh, irrepressible and thought provoking—musically, lyrically, conceptually. Distinguished by excessive speed (up-tempo grooves precisely executed), intensity and complexity in riffs and rhythm figures, ambitious arrangements and intricate formal structures fraught with multiple tempos, unusual modulations, meter changes and tonal ambiguity, precarious balances of sophistication and rawness in guitar soloing and socially conscious lyrics and imagery, one senses an overall conviction in both physical performance and artistic philosophy. Since thrash's inception, a handful of important groups have come to define and embody the new music: Anthrax, Exodus, Megadeth, Testament, M.O.D. and, of course, Metallica.

When Metallica released their debut album *Kill 'Em All* in 1984, they were emerging as a vital new voice in the underground Bay Area thrash movement. Guitarist/composer/vocalist James Hetfield and drummer/composer Lars Ulrich had moved up to the San Francisco vicinity to escape the confines of a dreary L.A. rock scene, comprised largely of Ratt's, Motley Crüe's and related spinoffs. There, they hooked up with bassist Cliff Burton and finally replaced guitarist Dave Mustaine (now with Megadeth) with the multi-faceted Kirk Hammett, just prior to the tracking of *Kill 'Em All*. The rest is history. Metallica has attained near-legendary status as the leading speed metal band of the 1980's—the fact reinforced by numerous sold-out concert appearances, a more than successful recording career and the unprecedented exposure in the genre (MTV, etc.).

All the signature devices which make Metallica's music so striking and immediately recognizable are well-displayed on *Kill 'Em All*. Their riffs are beyond heavy, delivered with a thick, distorted sound and the unmistakable downstroke attack of Hetfield and Hammett. Prime examples can be heard in the rhythm figures to practically any song on the record, with "The Four Horsemen" being particularly noteworthy. Compare the variety of approaches utilized: heavy palm muting of a simple but effective three-note riff against an E pedal (6th string open) in Rhy. Fig. 1, a muted, triplet E pedal "gallop" motif under power chords E5, D, C5 and G5 in Rhy. Fig. 2, sustaining power chords E5, D5, C5 and B5 in Rhy. Fig. 3, and the unusual E Phrygian mode alluded to in Rhy. Figs. 4 and 5. Rhy. Fig. 4 states this in no uncertain terms with a characteristic F5 to E5

chord move, and Rhy. Fig. 5 incorporates a C5—>C#5—>D5 chromatic progression into the E minor sound. The familiar tritone dissonance is present in the repertoire as expected. Check out the riffs in "Jump in the Fire" (Rhy. Fig. 2—tritone of Db against G), "Whiplash" (chorus: Rhy. Fig. 3—F# against C), "Metal Militia" (Rhy. Fig. 1—Bb against E and Rhy. Figs. 2 and 3—Eb5 against an A minor tonal center) and the intro to "Am I Evil?" where the E—>Bb relationship is presented in a number of ways: chordally in bars 5-7, and in single-note form in bars 13 and 14—foreshadowing its prominent harmonic role in the chorus.

Tempo changes? Naturally. The examples are plentiful. In "The Four Horsemen," a fast rock shuffle at ♩=204 changes to half time (Riff B) ♩=102 and then abruptly gives way to a faster straight-eighth feel at ♩=164. The latter two tempo changes are further complicated by a meter change of 4/4 to 2/4 to 4/4. Metallica handles them with an ease that is virtually telepathic. Consider also the various tempo fluctuations in "Am I Evil?" The intro begun moderately at ♩=100 proceeds to free time (one bar, conducted by feel) and then to a blistering speed of ♩=240. The verse, pre-chorus and chorus are at ♩=160, with Rhy. Fig. 4 picking up momentum to a faster triplet feel to ♩=192 for the bridge and guitar solo.

Feel changes and meter changes occur with such regularity that they must be perceived as idiomatic. Note the interesting use of three bars of 4/4 and one of 7/8 as a consistent rhythmic sequence in the chorus and solo of "Hit the Lights" (see the composite figure of Rhy. Fig. 3 plus Riff B in the solo). Other examples can be found in "Whiplash" (intro and solo), "Motorbreath" (going into Guitar solo I with a 5/4 bar and into Guitar solo II with a 2/4 bar) and within "Blitzkrieg" (Rhy. Fig. 1). "Phantom Lord" provides a clear-cut sample of the band's ability to change feel in the interlude between guitar solos, but the album as a whole is absolutely teeming with countless other similar events skillfully arranged and precisely executed in trademark Metallica fashion. It would be an invaluable experience to track them down for yourself. Start with "Whiplash," "No Remorse" and "The Four Horsemen."

Kirk Hammett's distinctive solos grace *Kill 'Em All* from one end to the other. His style is the fusion of a blues-based hard rock attitude a la Schenker, Aerosmith, Hendrix and Beck, with classically-tinged Euro-metal shadings (in the vein of Uli Roth and Randy Rhoads) and a fair portion of abstract modernism (no doubt fostered by close contact with teacher Joe Satriani). His well-known solos run the gamut from fast staccato and muted picked runs and legato scale lines to relentless repeating riffs (frequently involving open-string pull-offs), bluesy, emotional string bending and finger vibrato, and the mandatory 80's guitar mannerisms (two-handed tap-ons, neat noises and whammy bar tricks). Definitive solos occur in "Whiplash," "Seek and Destroy" and "Hit the Lights" (these feature some "outside" extended chromatic licks), "Phantom Lord" and "Motorbreath" (played with his familiar wah wah pedal tone) and "The Four Horsemen" with its quirky cross-relation dissonance of C-natural and C-sharp (note to chord relationship) in Guitar solo I. At this point in Kirk's career, he was based largely in the pentatonic and blues tonalities with brief, contrasting episodes of modality, chromaticism and ostinato incorporated into his soloing as thematic and melodic tangents.

- Wolf Marshall

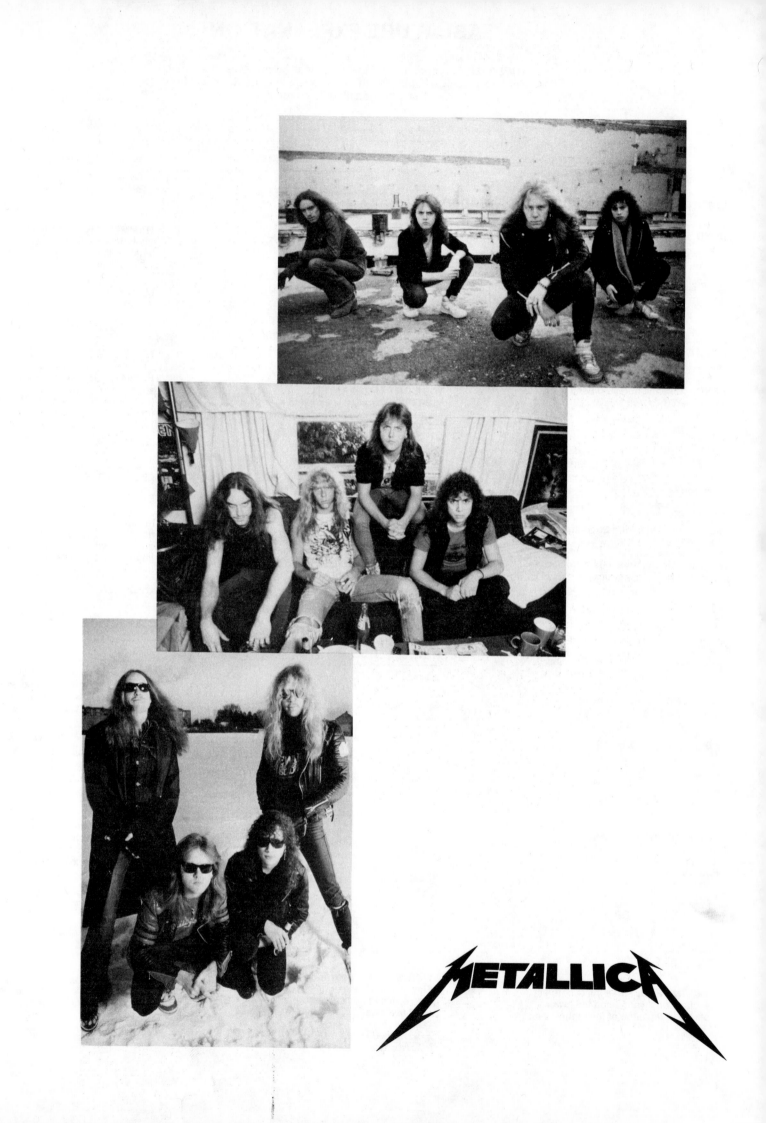

TABLATURE EXPLANATION

TABLATURE: A six-line staff that graphically represents the guitar fingerboard. By placing a number on the appropriate line, the string and fret of any note can be indicated. For example:

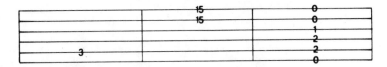

Definitions for Special Guitar Notation

BEND: Strike the note and bend up ½ step (one fret).

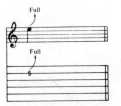

BEND: Strike the note and bend up a whole step (two frets).

BEND AND RELEASE: Strike the note and bend up ½ (or whole) step, then release the bend back to the original note. All three notes are tied, only the first note is struck.

PRE-BEND: Bend the note up ½ (or whole) step, then strike it.

PRE-BEND AND RELEASE: Bend the note up ½ (or whole) step. Strike it and release the bend back to the original note.

UNISON BEND: Strike the two notes simultaneously and bend the lower note up to the pitch of the higher.

VIBRATO: The string is vibrated by rapidly bending and releasing the note with the left hand or tremolo bar.

WIDE OR EXAGGERATED VIBRATO: The pitch is varied to a greater degree by vibrating with the left hand or tremolo bar.

SLIDE: Strike the first note and then slide the same left-hand finger up or down to the second note. The second note is not struck.

SLIDE: Same as above, except the second note is struck.

SLIDE: Slide up to the note indicated from a few frets below.

SLIDE: Strike the note and slide up or down an indefinite number of frets, releasing finger pressure at the end of the slide.

HAMMER-ON: Strike the first (lower) note, then sound the higher note with another finger by fretting it without picking.

HAMMER-ON: Without picking, sound the note indicated by sharply fretting the note with a left-hand finger.

PULL-OFF: Place both fingers on the notes to be sounded. Strike the first note and without picking, pull the finger off to sound the second (lower) note.

TRILL: Very rapidly alternate between the note indicated and the small note shown is parentheses by hammering on and pulling off.

TAPPING: Hammer ("tap") the fret indicated with the right-hand index or middle finger and pull off to the note fretted by the left hand.

PICK SLIDE: The edge of the pick is rubbed down the length of the string producing a scratchy sound.

pick slide

TREMOLO PICKING: The note is picked as rapidly and continuously as possible.

trem. pick

RAKE: Drag the pick across the strings indicated from low to high with a single downward motion.

rake

ARPEGGIO: Play the notes of the chord indicated by quickly rolling them from bottom to top.

NATURAL HARMONIC: Strike the note while the left hand lightly touches the string over the fret indicated.

Harm.

Harm.
12

ARTIFICIAL HARMONIC: The note is fretted normally and a harmonic is produced by adding the edge of the thumb or the tip of the index finger of the right hand to the normal pick attack. High volume or distortion will allow for a greater variety of harmonics.

A.H.
(8va)

9

A.H. pitch: E

TREMOLO BAR: The pitch of the note or chord is dropped a specified number of steps then returned to the original pitch.

1¼

trem. bar
1¼

5

PALM MUTING: The note is partially muted by the right hand lightly touching the string(s) just before the bridge.

P.M. - - - - - - - - - - - - -|

0   0   0   0

MUFFLED STRINGS: A percussive sound is produced by laying the left hand across the strings without depressing them and striking them with the right hand.

RHYTHM SLASHES: Strum chords in rhythm indicated. Use chord voicings found in the fingering diagrams at the top of the first page of the transcription.

Am   D

RHYTHM SLASHES (SINGLE NOTES): Single notes can be indicated in rhythm slashes. The circled number above the note name indicates which string to play. When successive notes are played on the same string, only the fret numbers are given.

⑤ 3fr.   2fr.   open   ⑥ 3fr.
C   B   A   G

efinitions of Musical Symbols

	Play an octave higher than written	. (staccato)	Play note short
na	Play two octaves higher than written	/	Repeat previous beat (used for quarter or eighth notes)
	Play as written	//	Repeat previous beat (used for sixteenth notes)
(pianissimo)	Very soft	⁒.	Repeat previous measure
iano)	Soft	‖: :‖	Repeat measures between repeat signs
(mezzo - piano)	Moderately soft		
(mezzo - forte)	Moderately loud	1. 2.	When a repeated section has different endings, play the first ending only the first time and the second ending only the second time.
forte)	Loud	‖: :‖	
(fortissimo)	Very loud		
accent)	Accentuate note (play it louder)	D.S. al Coda	Go back to the sign (𝄋), then play until the measure marked "To Coda," then skip to the section labeled "Coda."
accent)	Accentuate note with great intensity	D.C. al Fine	Go back to the beginning of the song and play until the measure marked "Fine" (end).

TE: Tablature numbers in parentheses mean:

1. The note is being sustained over a barline (note in standard notation is tied), or

2. The note is sustained, but a new articulation (such as a hammer-on, pull-off, slide or vibrato) begins, or

3. The note is a barely audible "ghost" note (note in standard notation is also in parentheses).

HIT THE LIGHTS

Words and Music by James Hetfield
and Lars Ulrich

1. No life till leath-er. ___ We're gon-na kick some ass ___ to-night.
2.3. *See additional lyrics*

Got the met-al mad-ness. When our fans start scream-in' it's right. Well al-

right, ___ yeah. ___ When we start to rock ___ we

nev-er ___ will stop a-gain. ___ Hit the ___

lights. Hit the ___ lights. ___

Fill 1 (end of Interlude I)

Fill 2 (end of Interlude II)

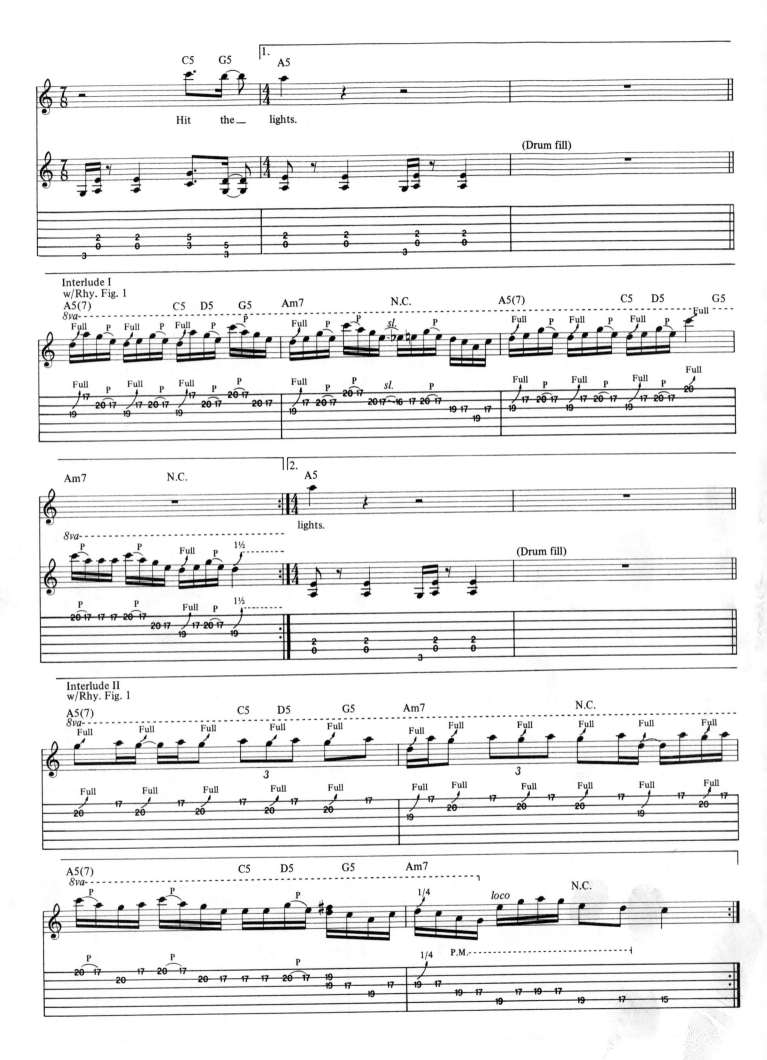

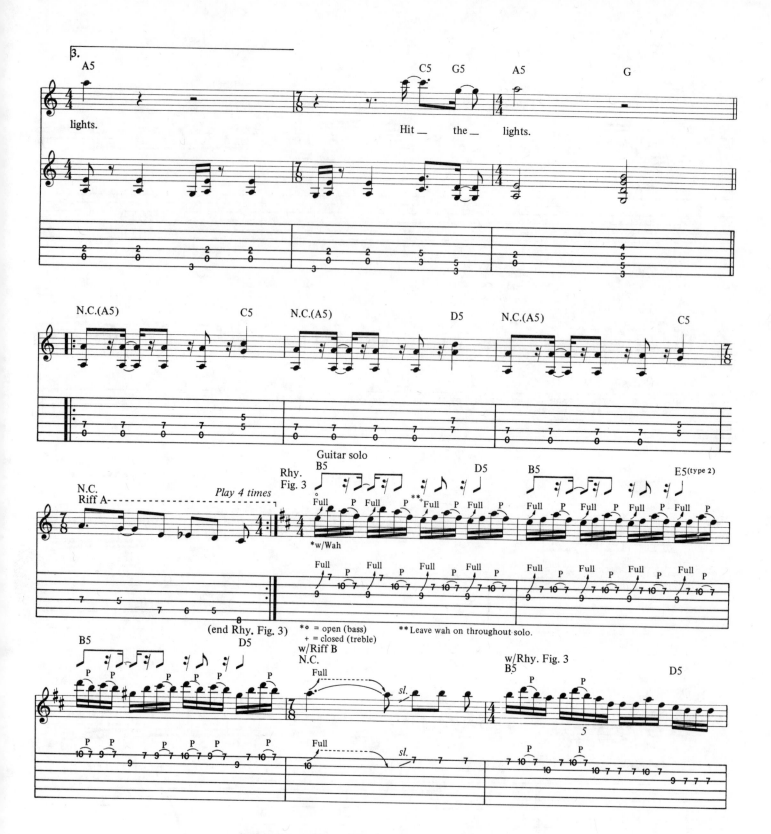

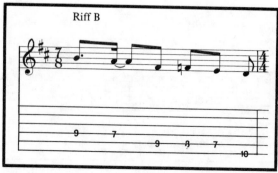

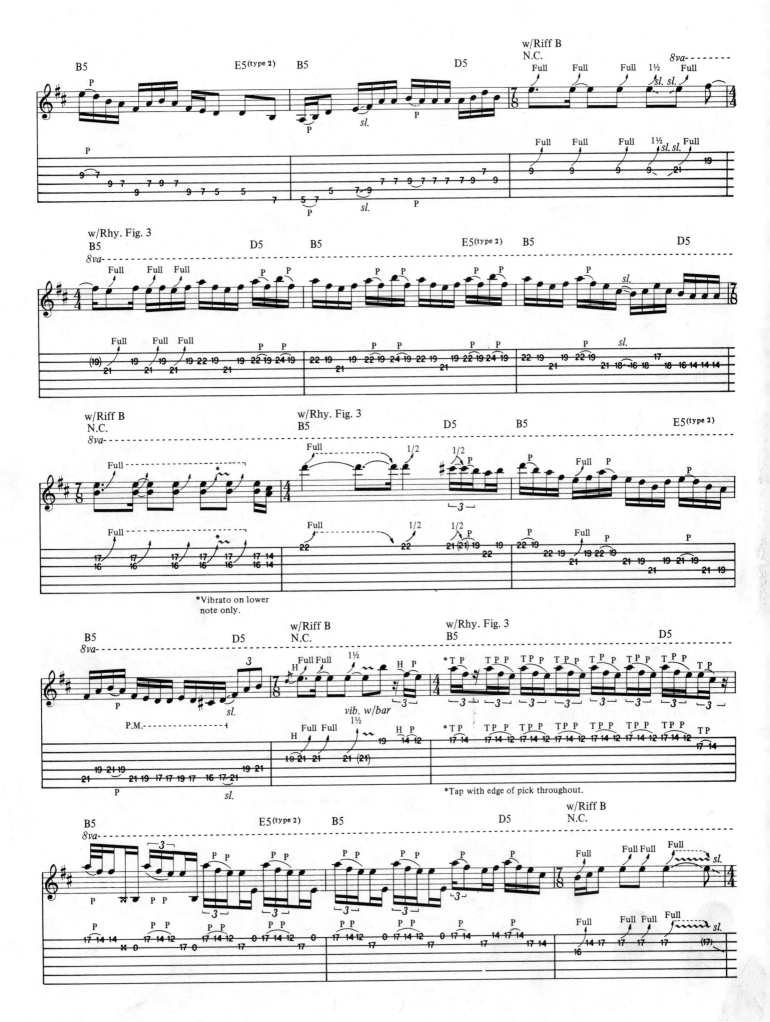

*Vibrato on lower note only.

*Tap with edge of pick throughout.

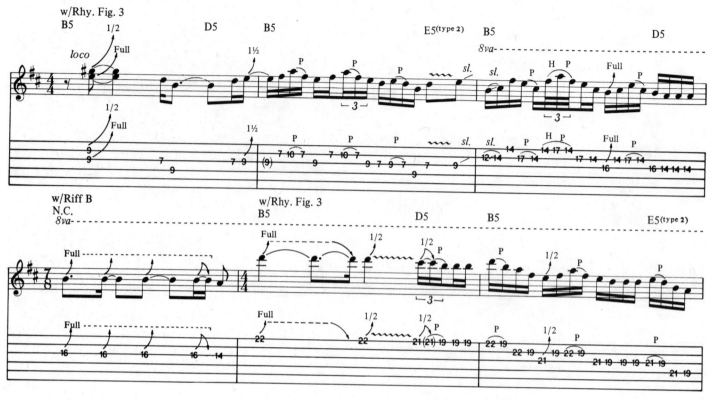

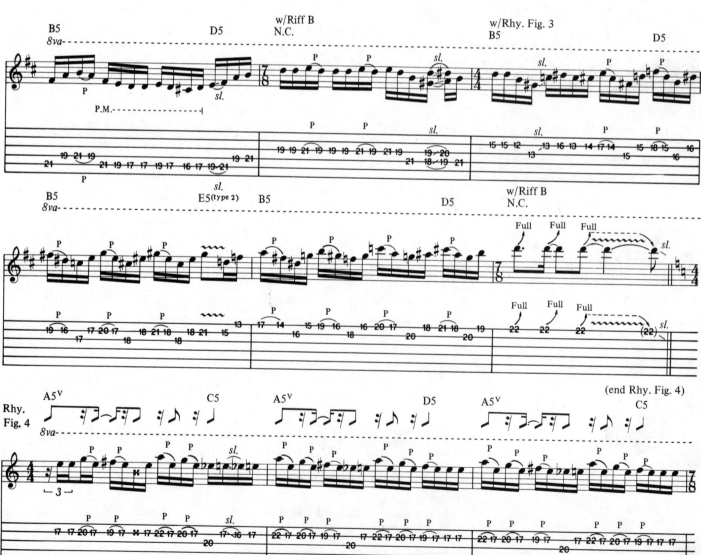

Additional Lyrics

2. Know our fans are insane.
   We're gonna blow this place away
   With volume higher
   Than anything today. The only way.
   When we start to rock we never, *etc.*

3. With all out screamin'
   We're gonna rip right through your brain.
   We got the lethal power.
   It's causin' you sweet pain. Oh sweet pain.
   When we start to rock we never, *etc.*

THE FOUR HORSEMEN

Words and Music by James Hetfield,
Lars Ulrich and Dave Mustaine

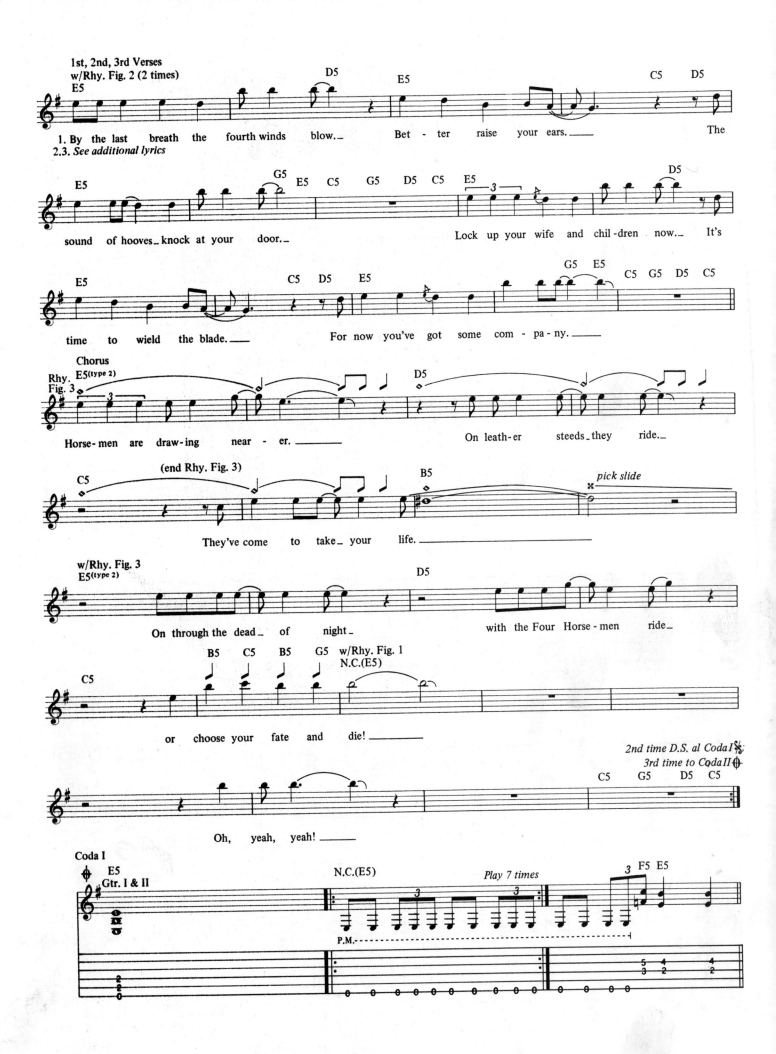

Time has tak-en its toll— on you.— The lines that crack— your face.—

Fam-ine, your bod-y it has torn through.— With-ered in ev-'ry place.—

Pes-ti-lence, for what you had to en-dure.— For what you have put oth-ers through.— Death, de-liv-'rance for

you for sure.— Now there's noth-ing you can do.—

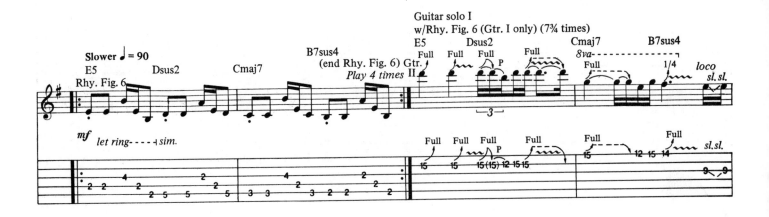

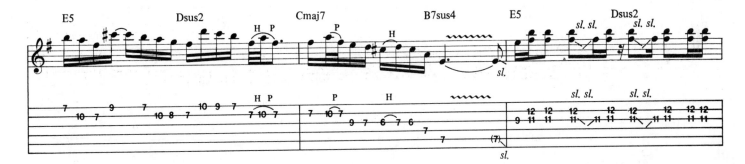

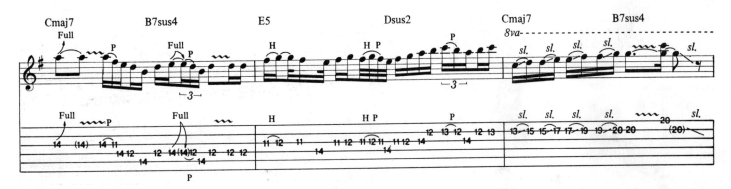

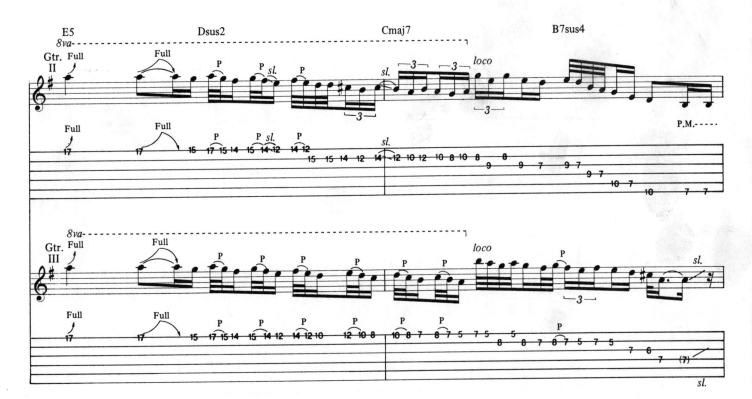

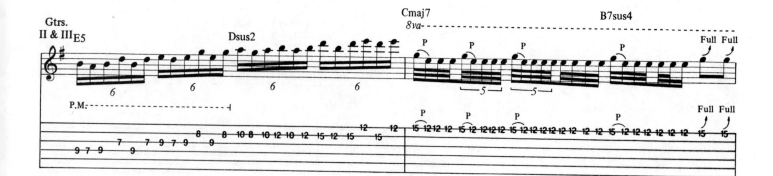

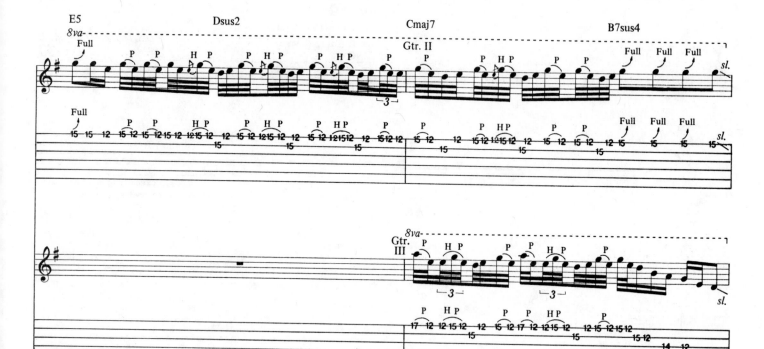

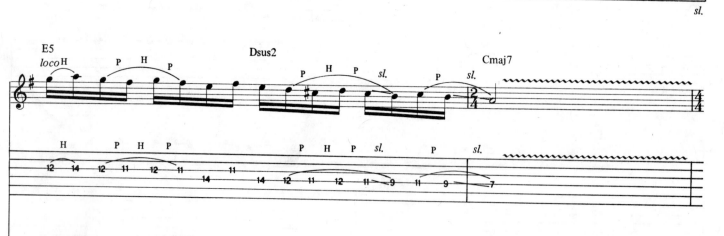

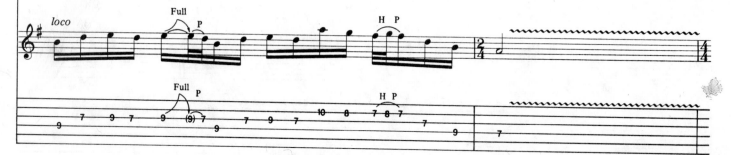

*Gtr. I: Depress bar after pull-off.
Gtr. II: Depress bar on first beat.
**Gtr. I indicated to right of slash in TAB.

*Can be approximated by steadily lowering
pitch of open low E string w/bar.

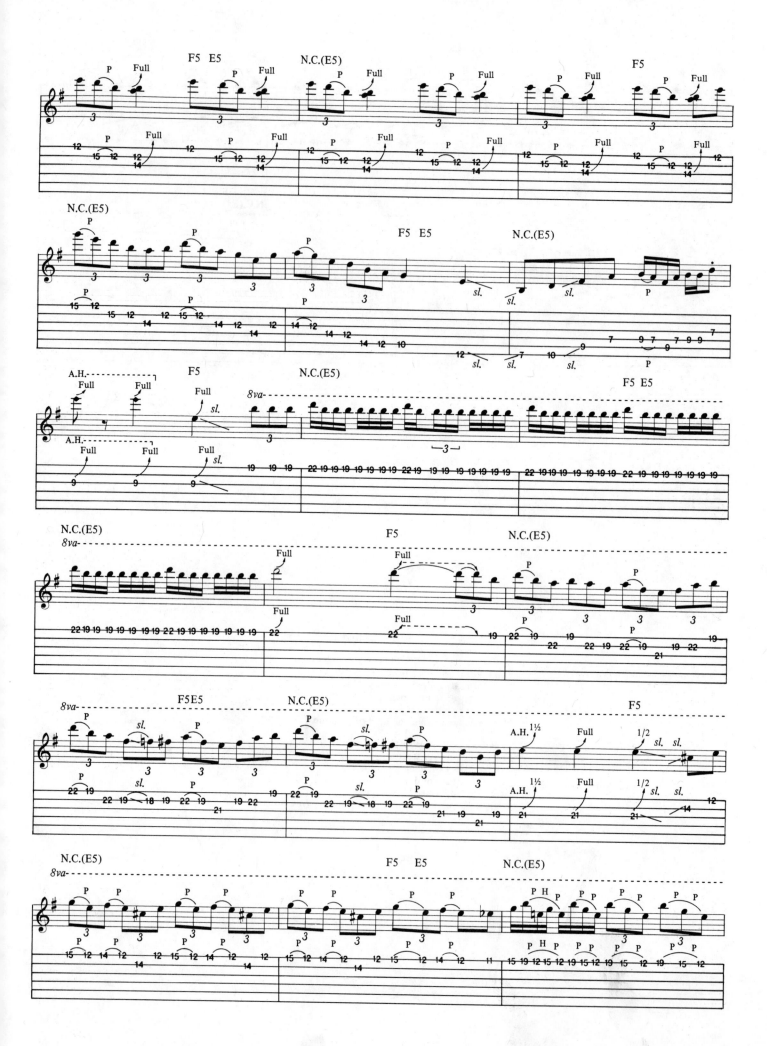

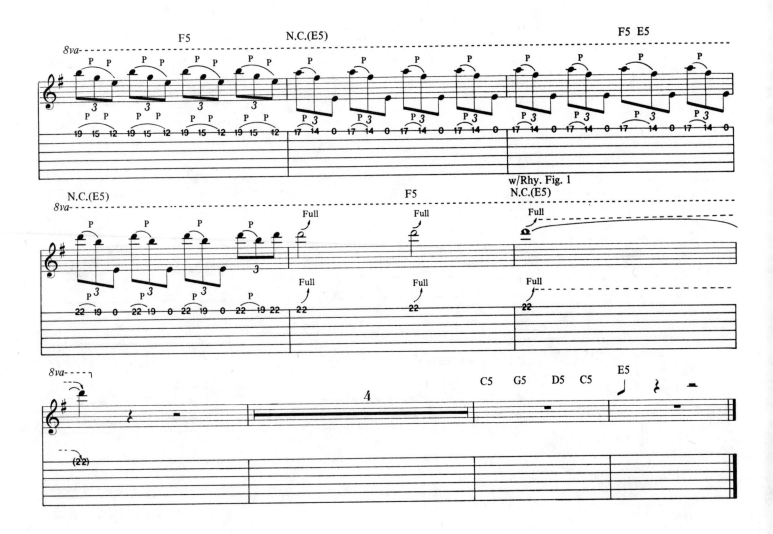

Additional Lyrics

2. You've been dying since the day you've been born.
   You know it's all been planned.
   The quartet of deliverance rides.
   A sinner once, a sinner twice,
   No need for confession now.
   'Cause now you've got the fight of your life. *(To Coda)*

3. So gather round young warriors now
   And saddle up your steeds.
   Killing scores with demon swords.
   Now is the death of doers of wrong.
   Swing the judgment hammer down.
   Safely inside armor, blood, guts and sweat. *(To Chorus)*

MOTORBREATH

Words and Music by James Hetfield

1. Liv-ing and dy-ing, laugh-ing and cry-ing. Once you have seen it you'll nev-er be the same.
2.3. *See additional lyrics*

Life in the fast lane is just how it seems. Hard and it's heav-y, it's dirt-y and mean.

Mo-tor - breath.__ It's how I live my life.

I can't take it an - y oth - er way. Mo-tor - breath.__ The

sign of liv - ing fast.__ It is go - ing to take your breath a - way.

N.C.
Riff A

*o = open (bass)
+ = closed (treble)

**Leave Wah on throughout solo.

Rhy. Fig. 2 (Gtrs. I & II)

24

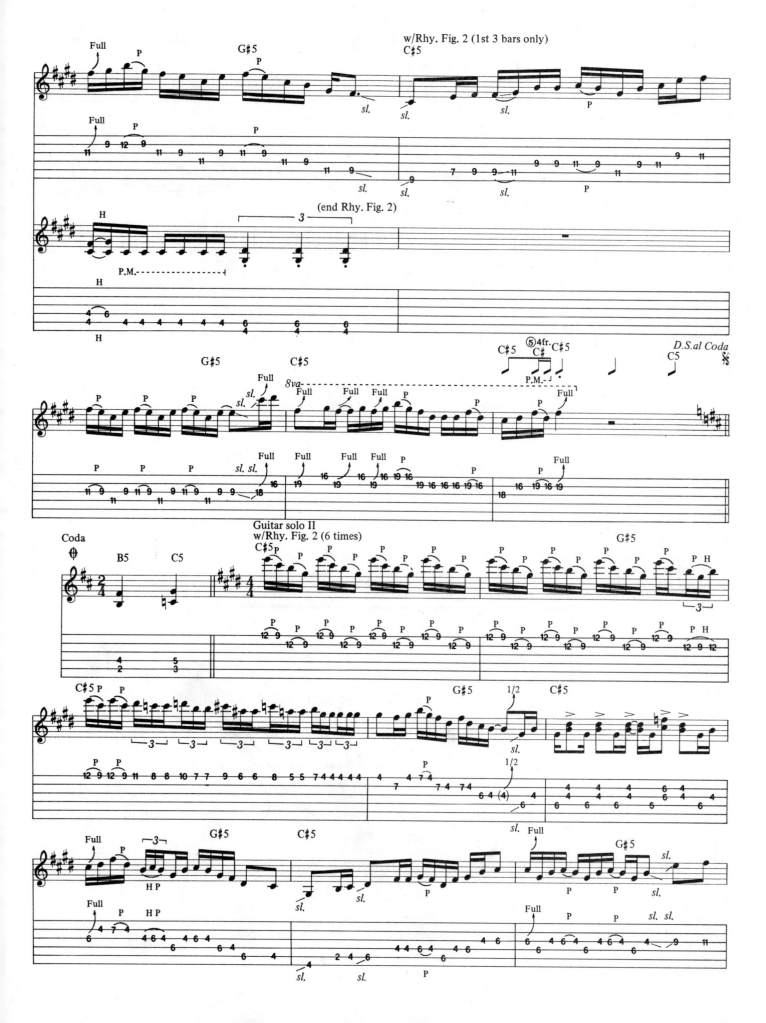

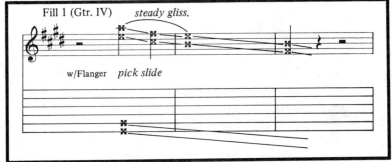

Additional Lyrics

2. Don't stop for nothin', it's full speed or nothin'.
   I'm takin' down you know whatever's in my way.
   Getting your kicks as you're shooting the line.
   Sending the shivers up and down my spine. *(To Chorus)*

3. Those people who tell you not to take chances,
   They are all missing on what life's about.
   You only live once so take hold of the chance.
   Don't end up like others, same song and dance. *(To Chorus)*

(ANESTHESIA) — PULLING TEETH

Music by Cliff Burton

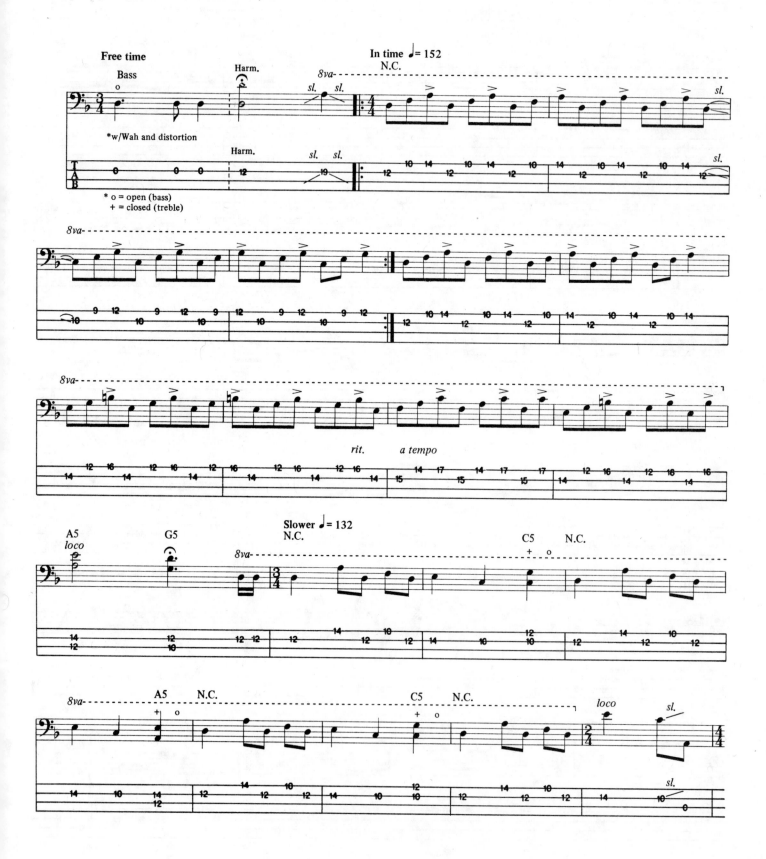

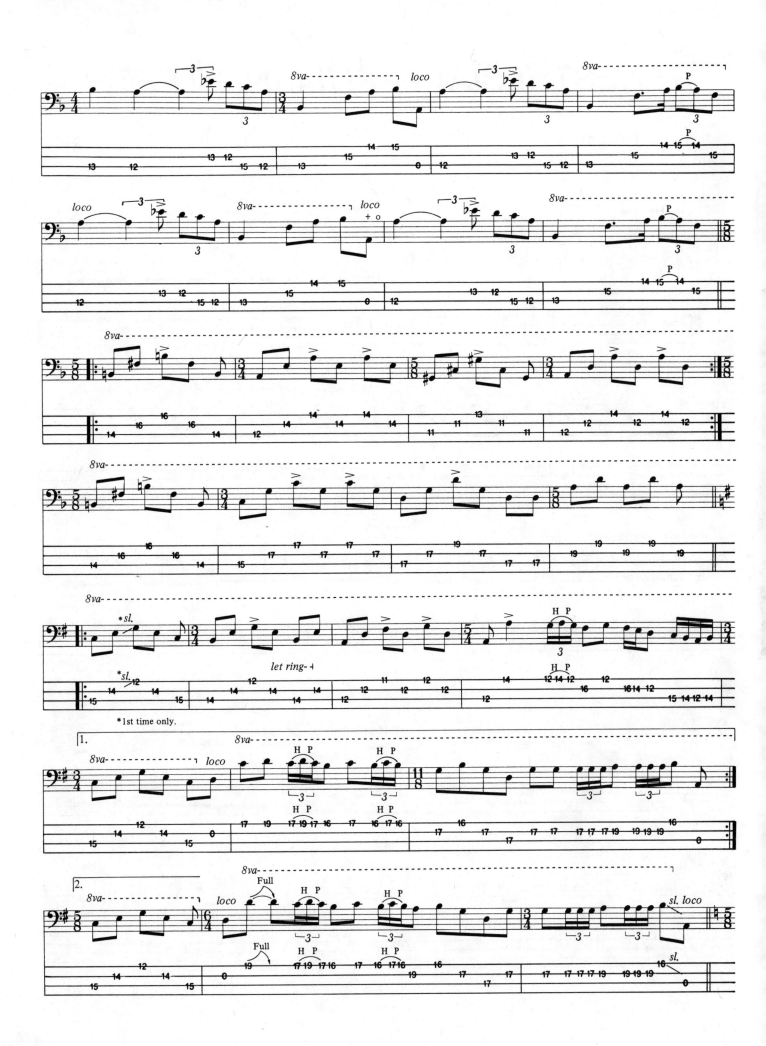

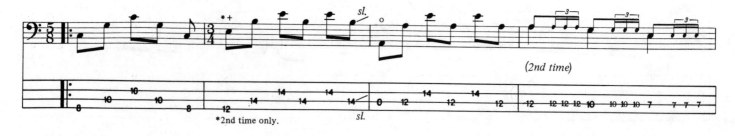

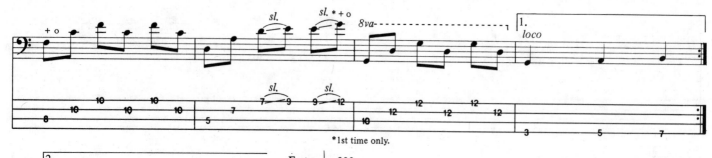

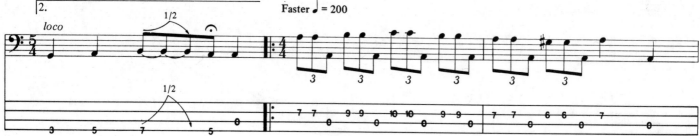

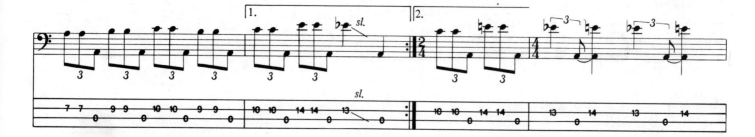

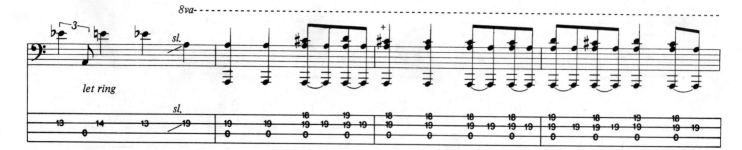

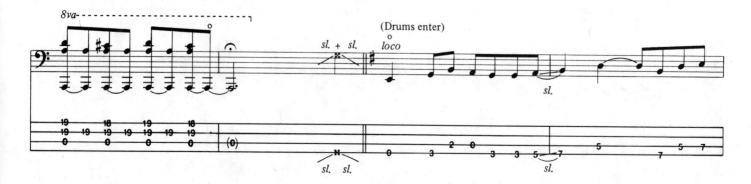

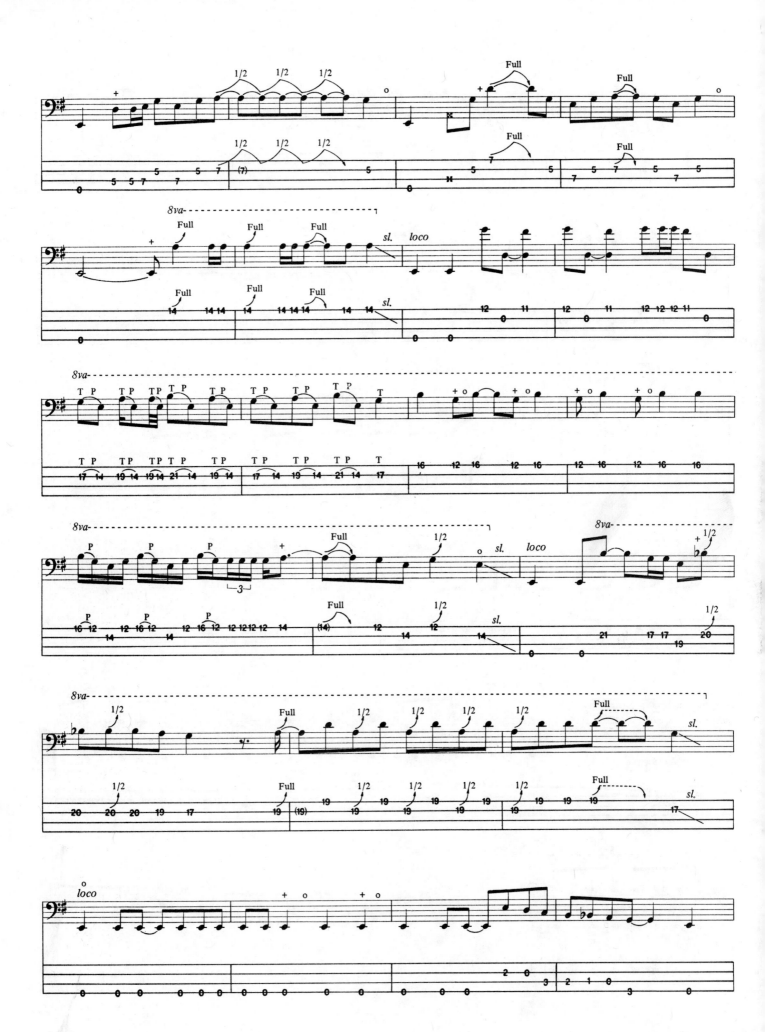

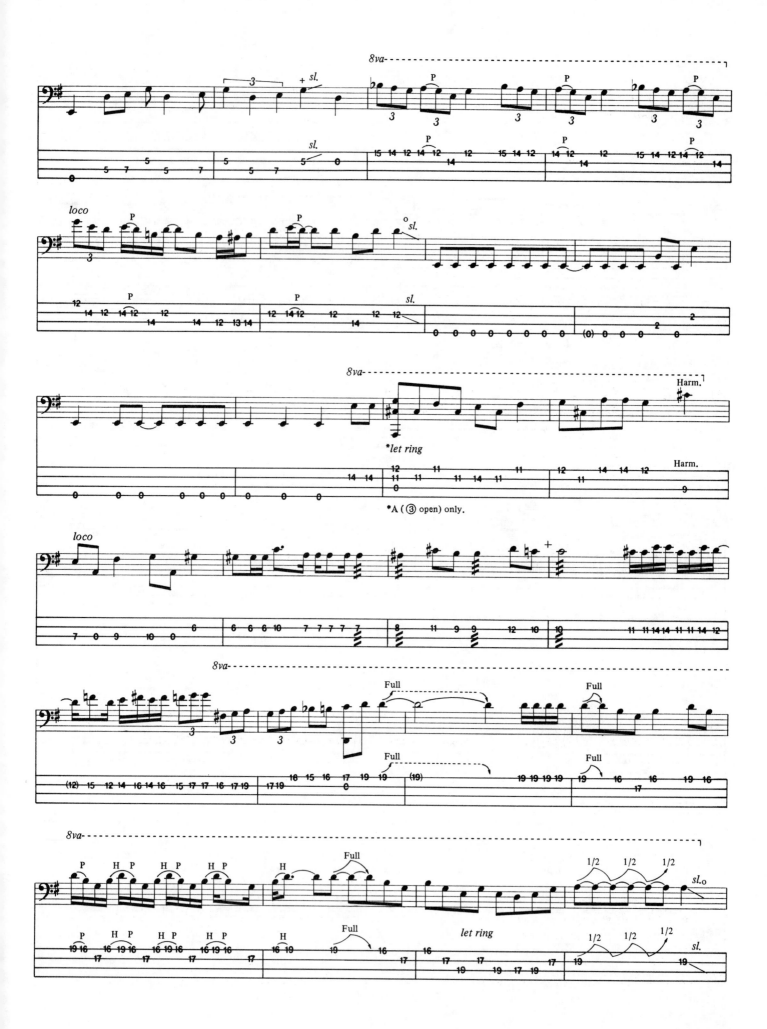

*Drag R.H. nails along E and A strings starting at 1st fret.

*Tap open D and G strings against pickups in rhythm indicated.

*Nail scrape

Seque: "Whiplash"

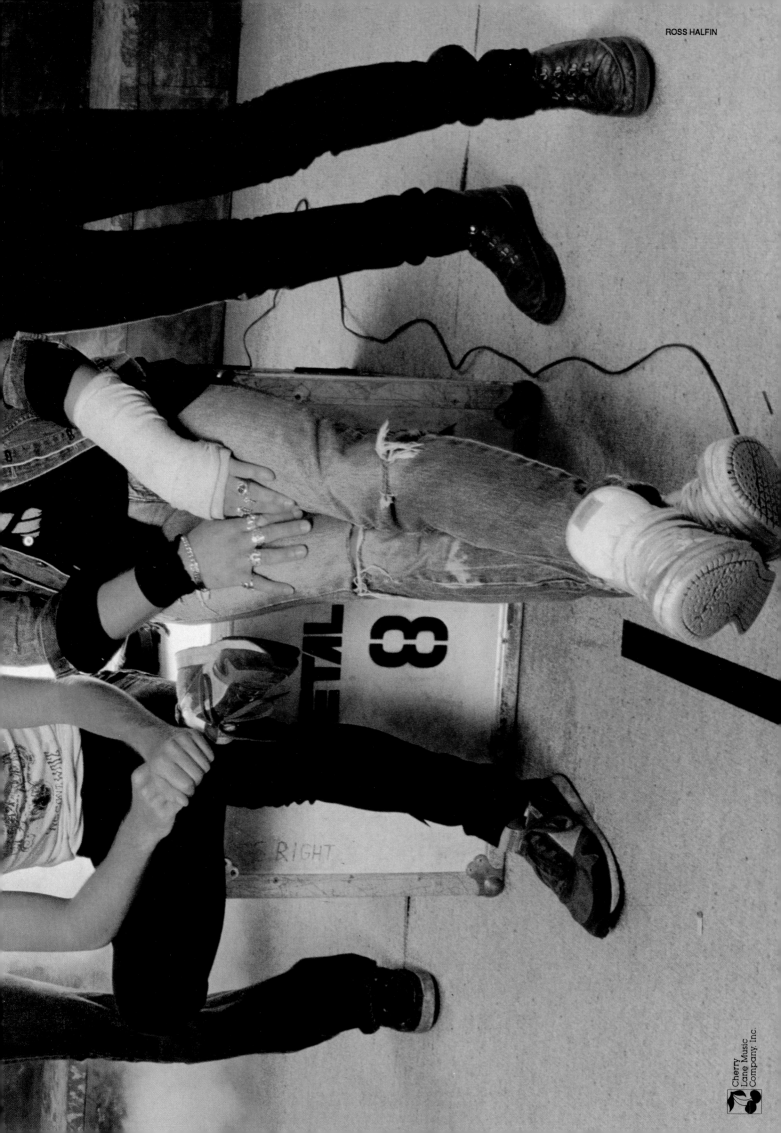

ROSS HALFIN

Cherry
Lane Music
Company, Inc.

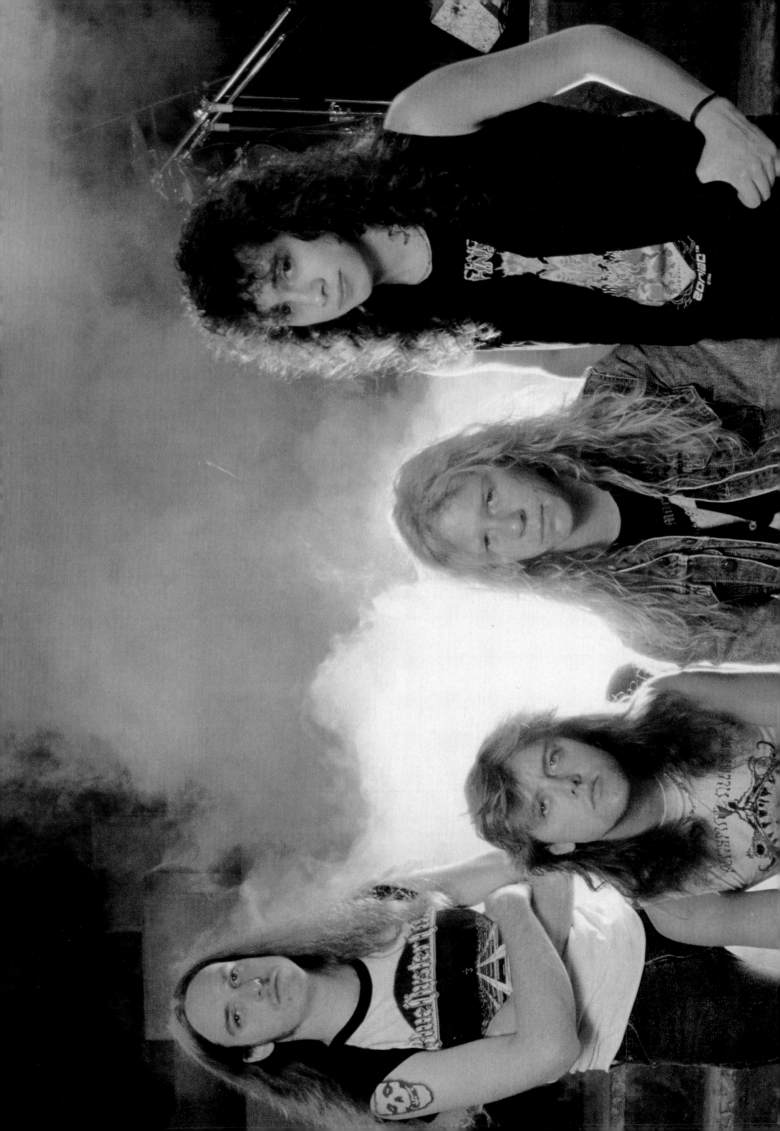

JUMP IN THE FIRE

Moderate Rock ♩ = 176

Words and Music by James Hetfield,
Lars Ulrich and Dave Mustaine

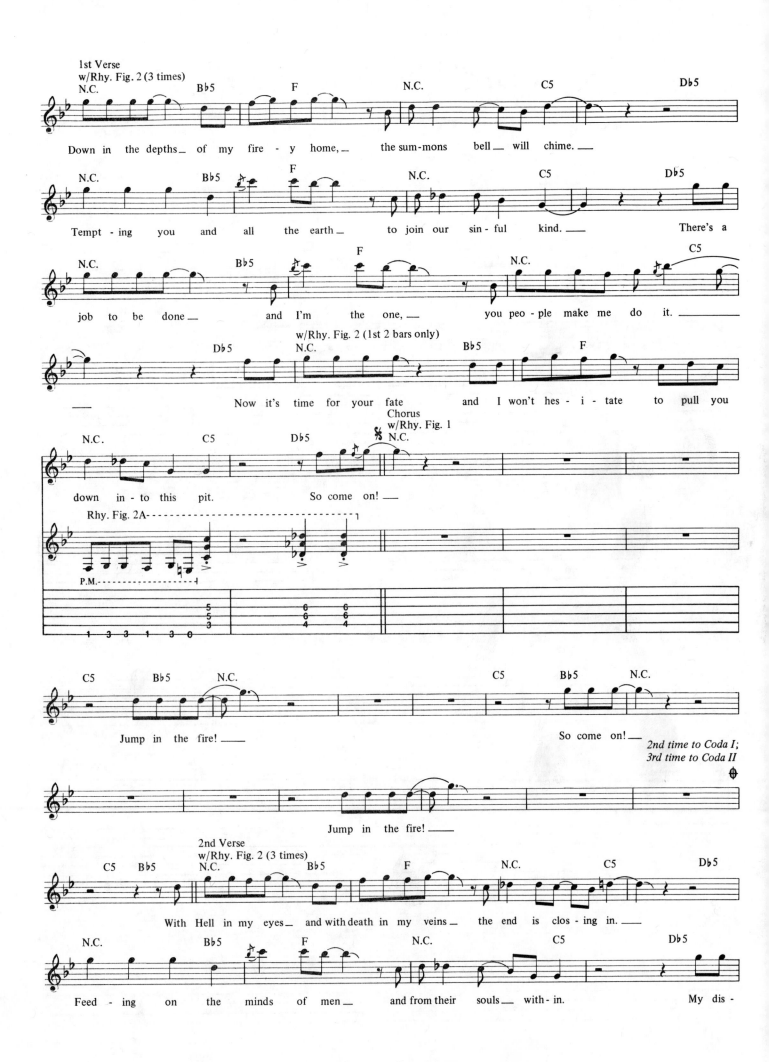

ci - ples all shout__ to search you out__ and they al-ways shall o - bey._____ Fol - low

me now, my child,__ not the meek or the mild,__ but do just as I say. So come on!__

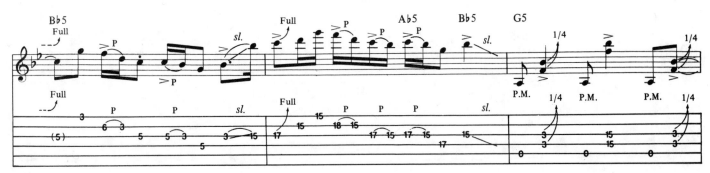

3rd Verse
w/Rhy. Fig. 2 (3 times)

Jump by your will __ or be tak-en by force, __ I'll get you ei - ther way. __

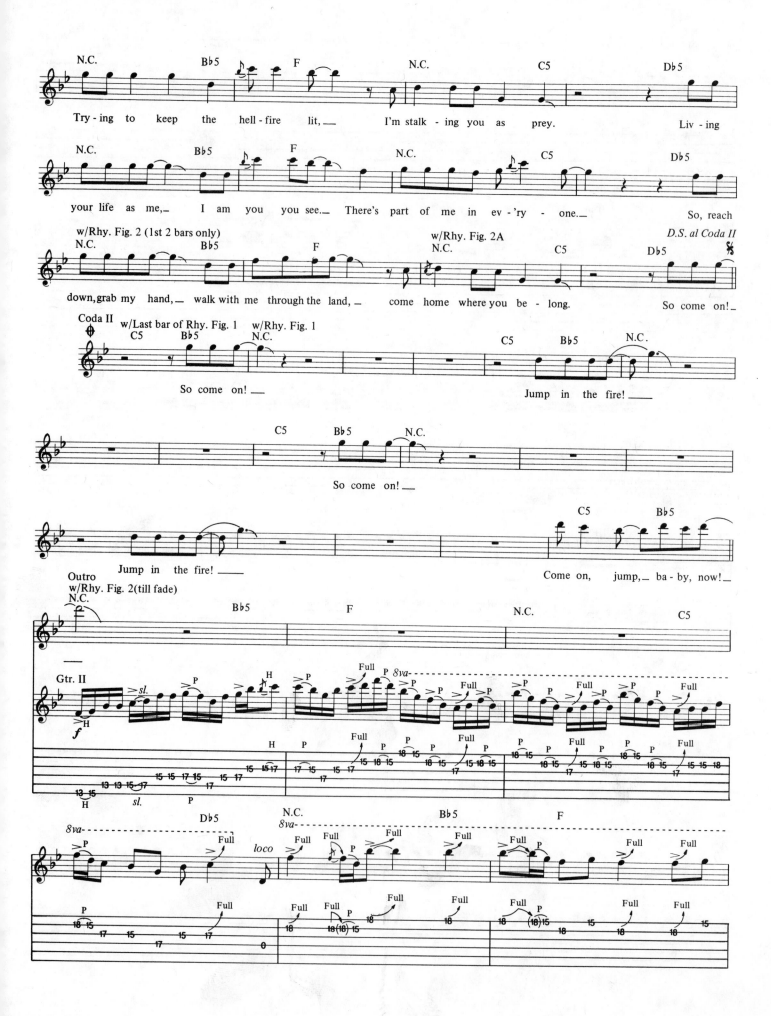

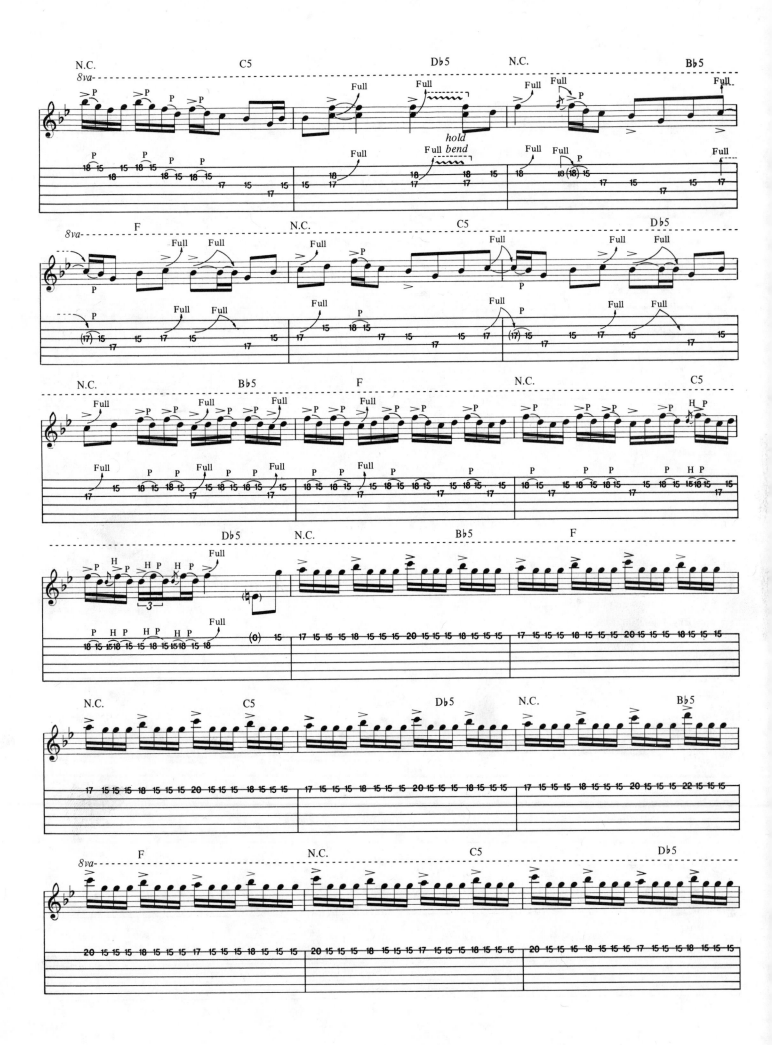

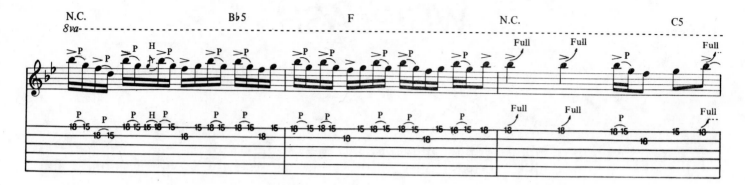

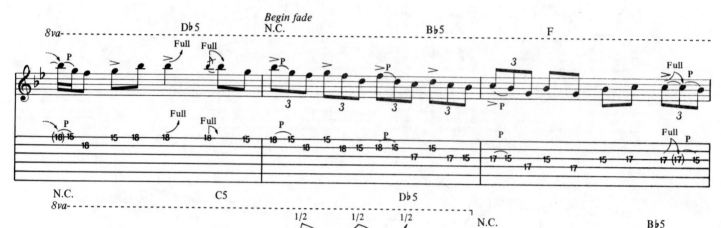

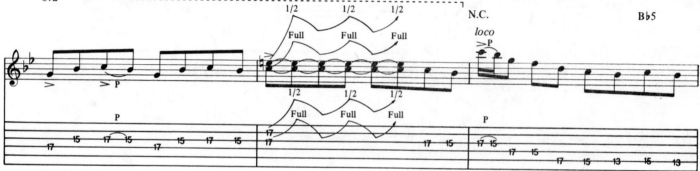

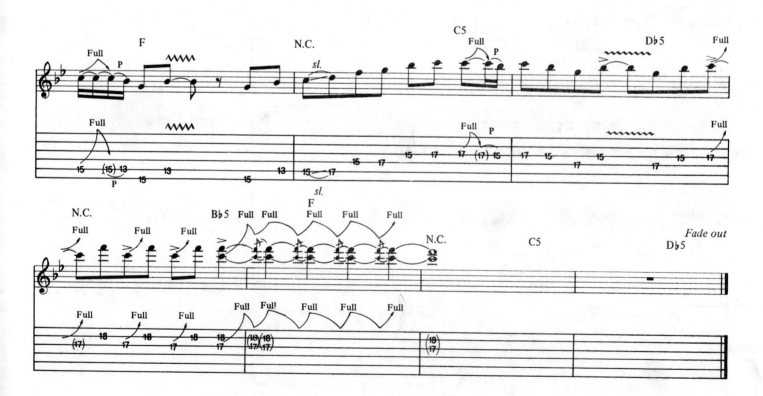

WHIPLASH

Words and Music by James Hetfield
and Lars Ulrich

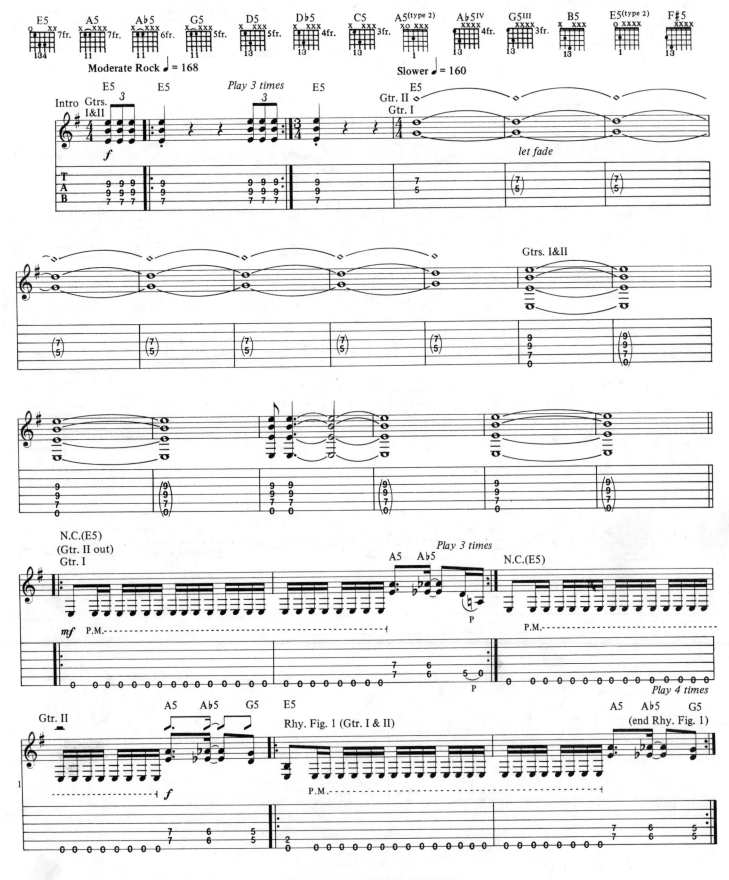

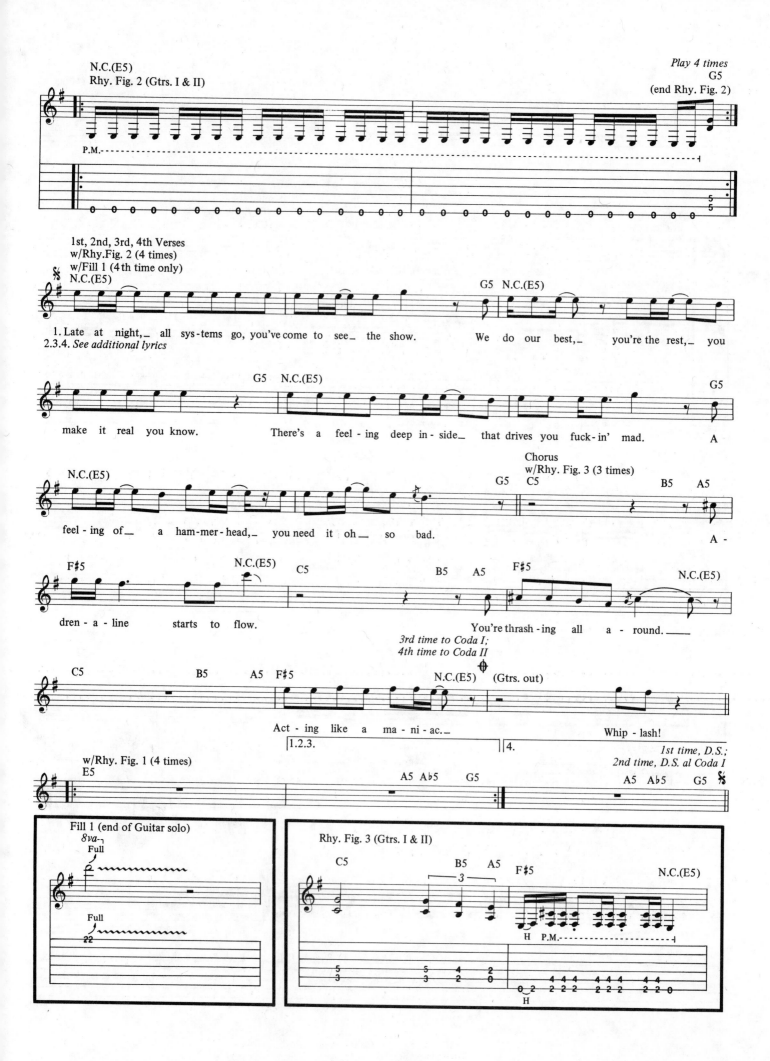

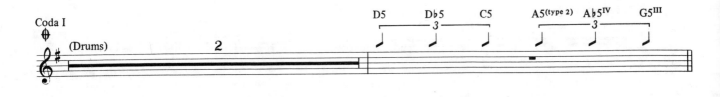

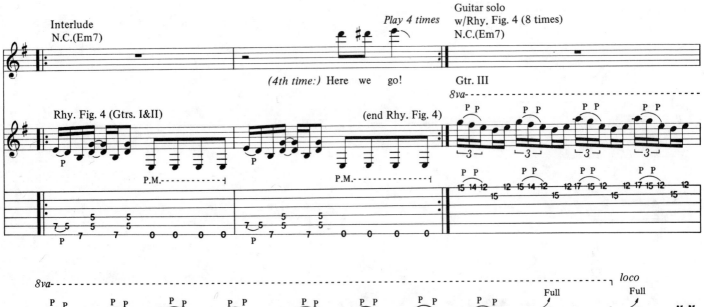

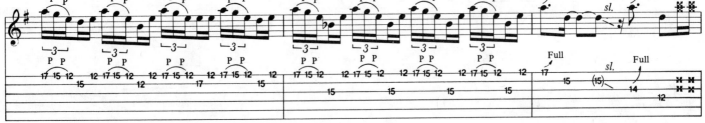

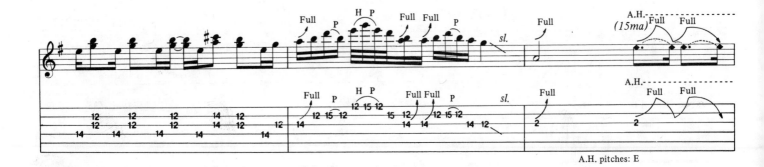

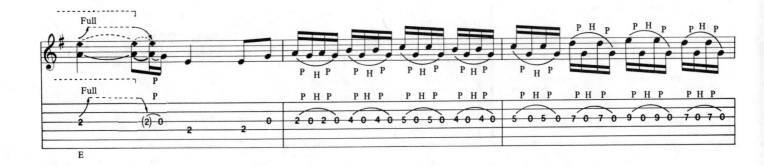

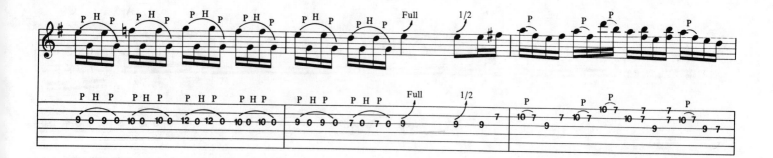

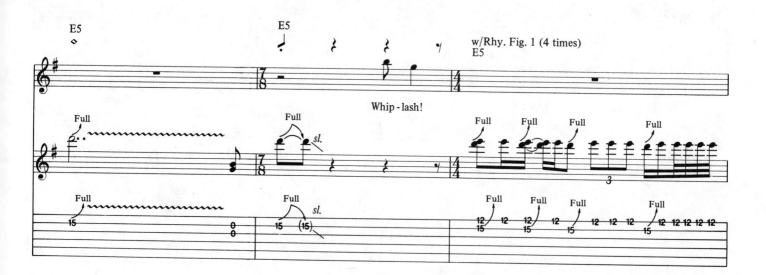

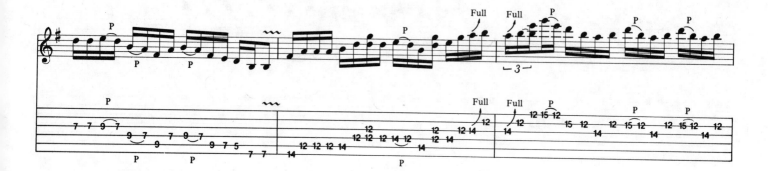

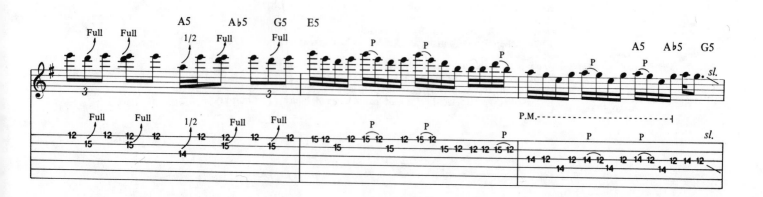

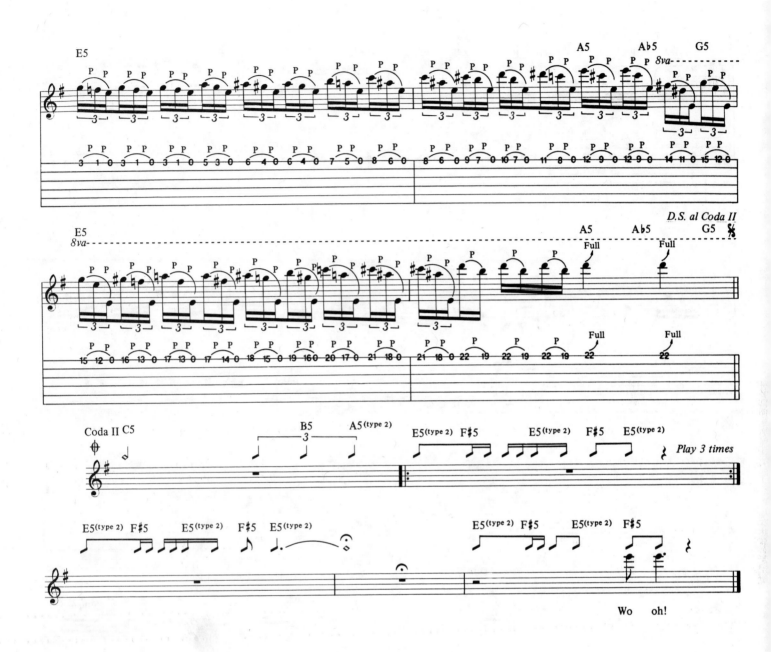

Additional Lyrics

2. Bang your head against the stage like you never did before.
   Make it ring, make it bleed, make it really sore.
   In a frenzied madness with your leather and your spikes,
   Heads are bobbing around, it's hot as hell tonight. *(To Chorus)*

3. Here on stage the Marshall noise is piercing through your ears.
   It kicks your ass, kicks your face, exploding feeling nears.
   Now's the time to let it rip, to let it fuckin' loose.
   We're gathered here to maim and kill 'cause this is what we choose. *(To Chorus)*

4. Show is through, the metal's gone, it's time to hit the road.
   Another town, another gig, again we will explode.
   Hotel rooms and motorways, life out here is raw.
   But we'll never stop, we'll never quit 'cause we're Metallica. *(To Chorus)*

PHANTOM LORD

Words and Music by James Hetfield,
Lars Ulrich and Dave Mustaine

45

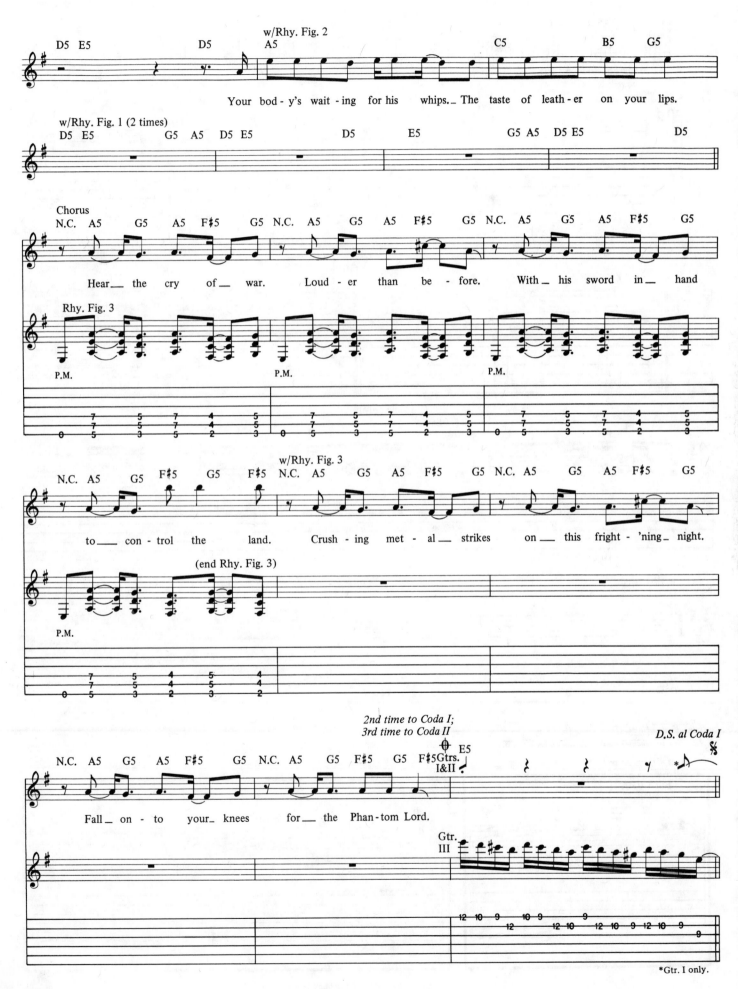

*Gtr. I only.

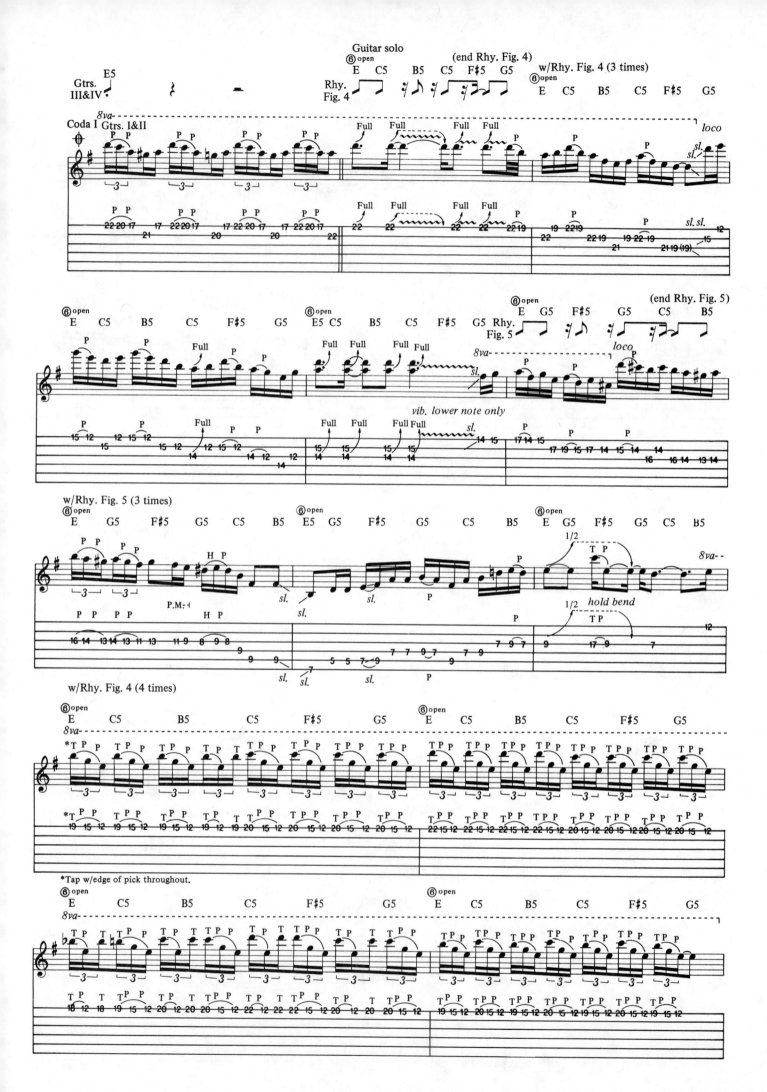

*Downstemmed notes indicated to right of
slash in TAB.
**Vib. refers to Gtrs. III & IV only.

*First time only, Gtrs. I & II
play first note of bar (E).

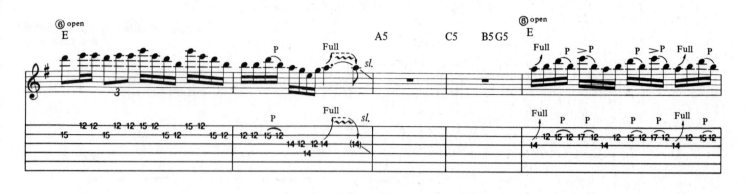

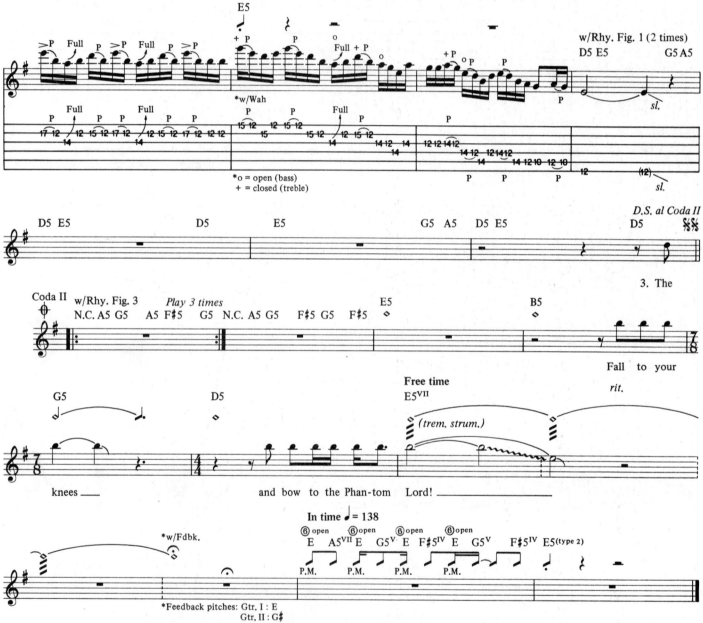

Additional Lyrics

2. Victims falling under chains,
   You hear them crying dying pains.
   Fists of terror breaking through,
   Now there's nothing you can do. *(To Chorus)*

3. The leathered armies have prevailed,
   The Phantom Lord has never failed.
   Smoke is lifting from the ground,
   The rising volume metal sound. *(To Chorus)*

NO REMORSE

Words and Music by James Hetfield
and Lars Ulrich

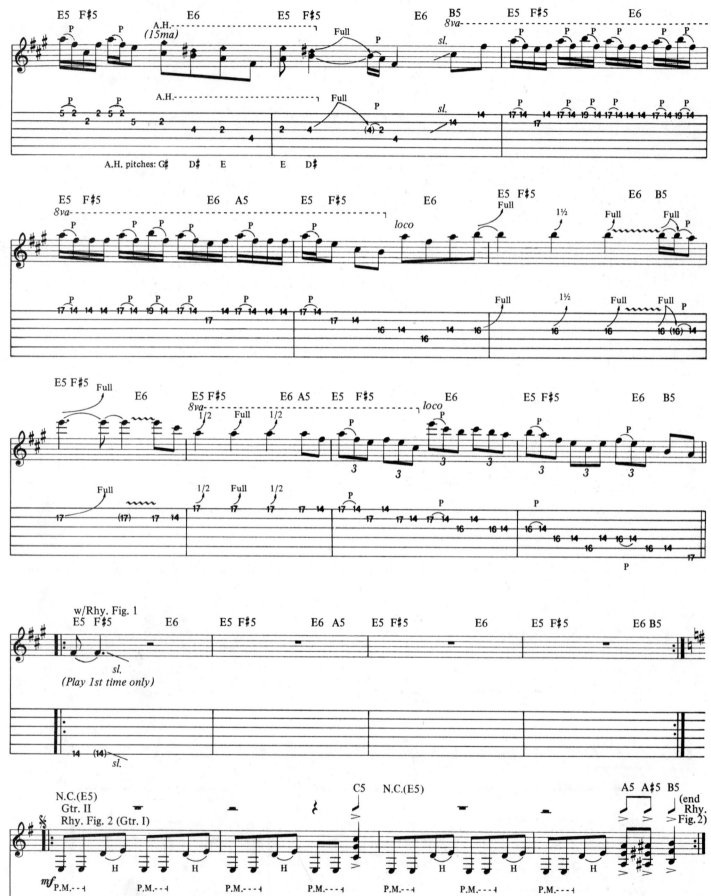

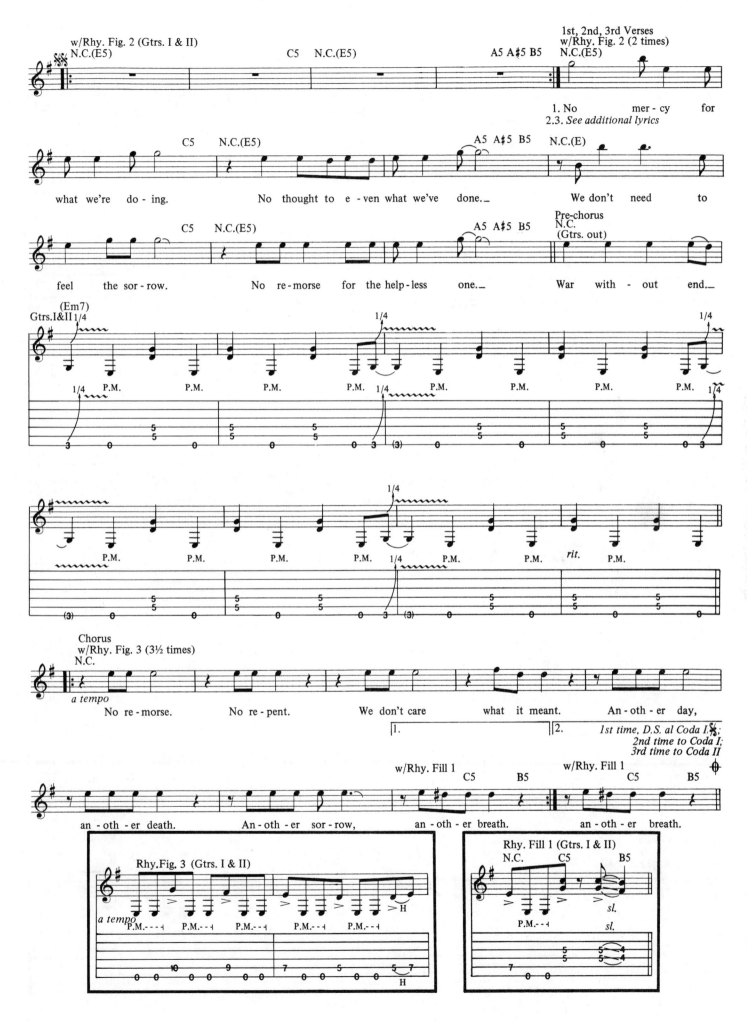

*Pick scrapes. While left hand mutes strings,
edge of pick is used to scrape up and down
approximately over middle pickup.

*Straight 8ths

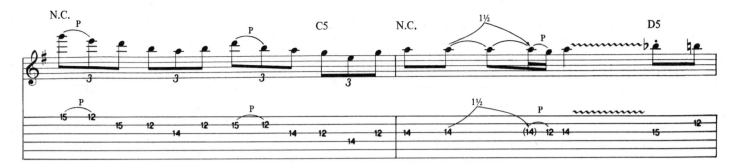

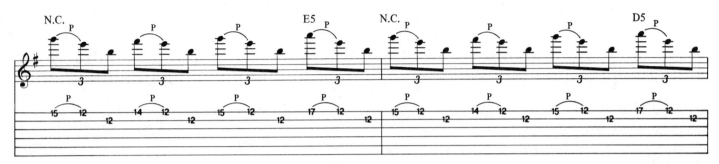

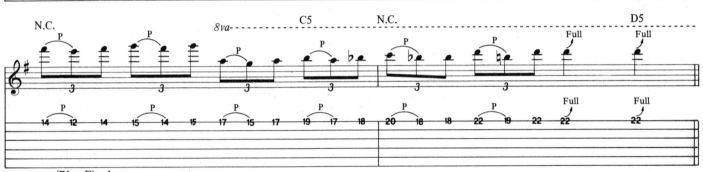

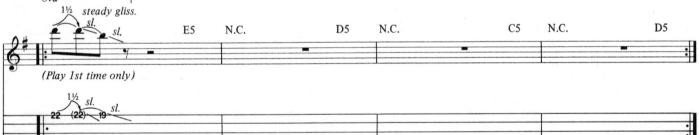

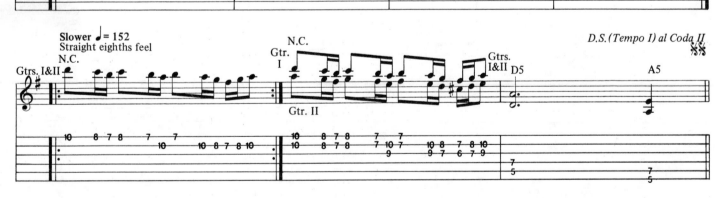

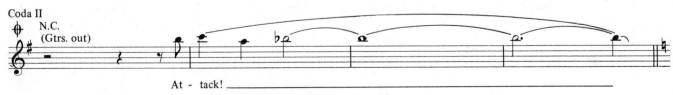

At - tack! _____

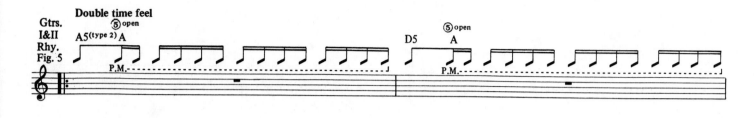

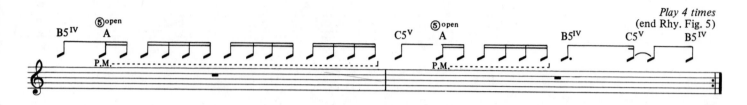

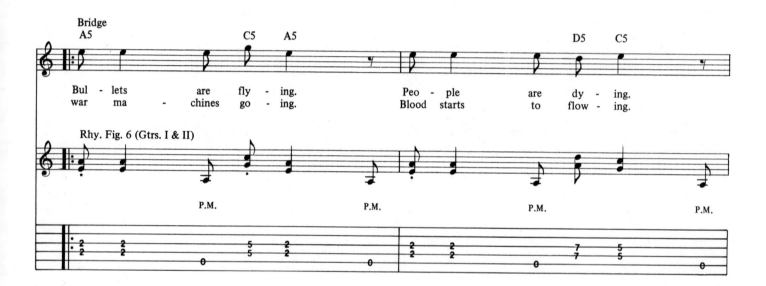

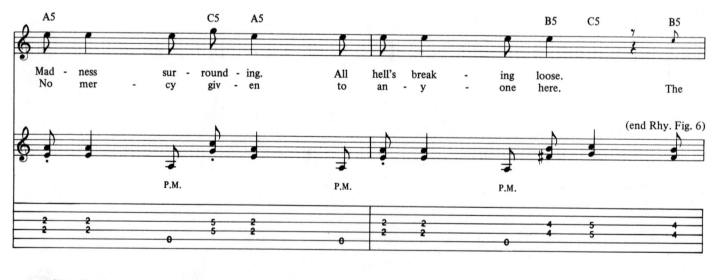

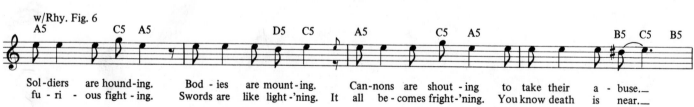

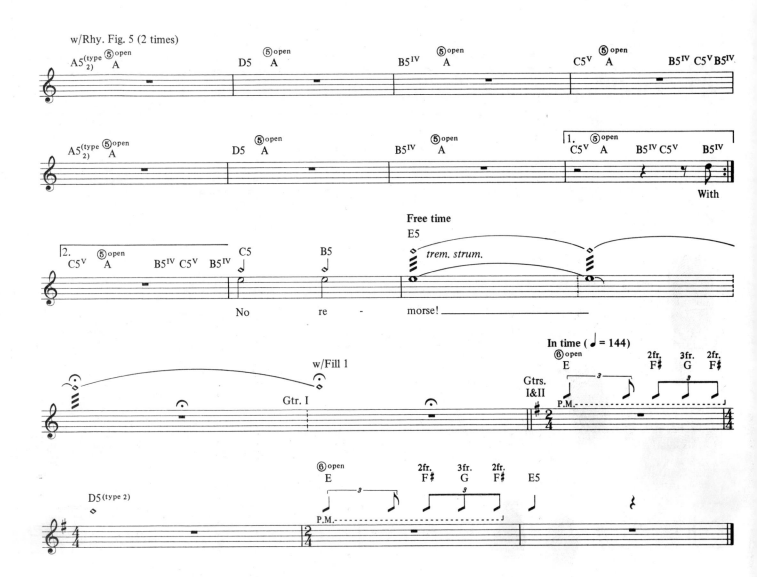

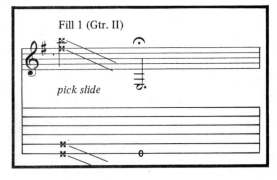

Fill 1 (Gtr. II)

pick slide

Additional Lyrics

2. Blood feeds the war machine
   As it eats a way across the land.
   We don't need to feel the sorrow.
   No remorse is the one command. *(To Pre-chorus)*

3. Only the strong survive.
   No will to save the weaker race.
   We're ready to kill all comers.
   Like a loaded gun right at your face. *(To Pre-chorus)*

SEEK & DESTROY

Words and Music by James Hetfield
and Lars Ulrich

57

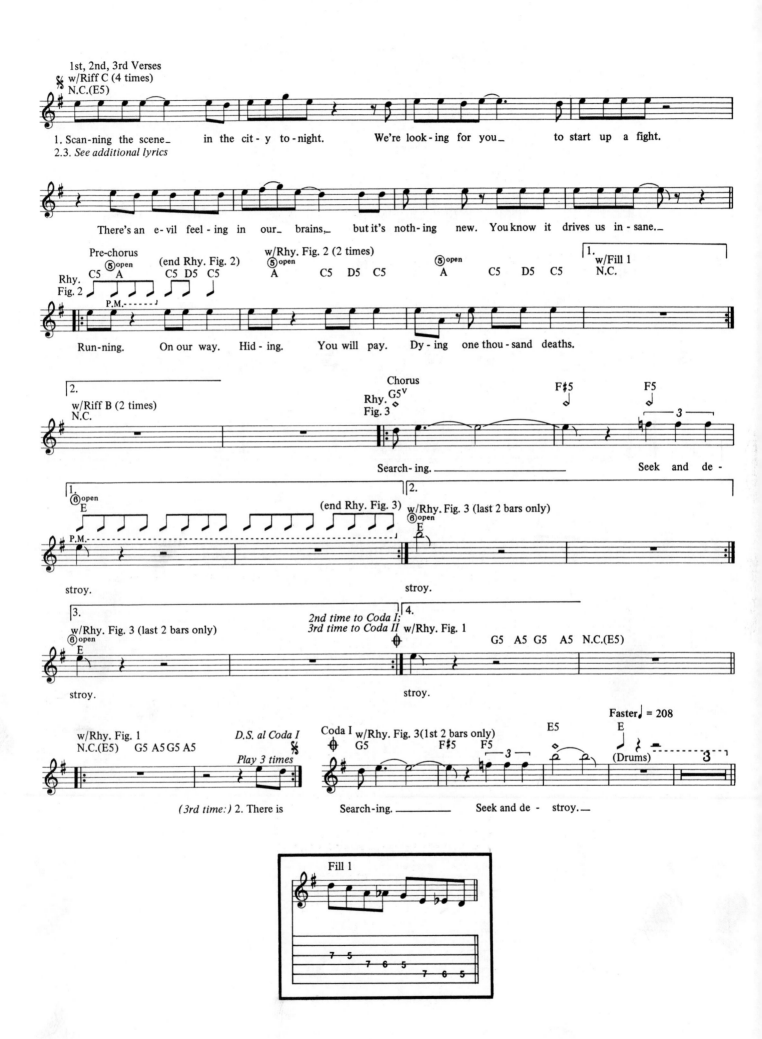

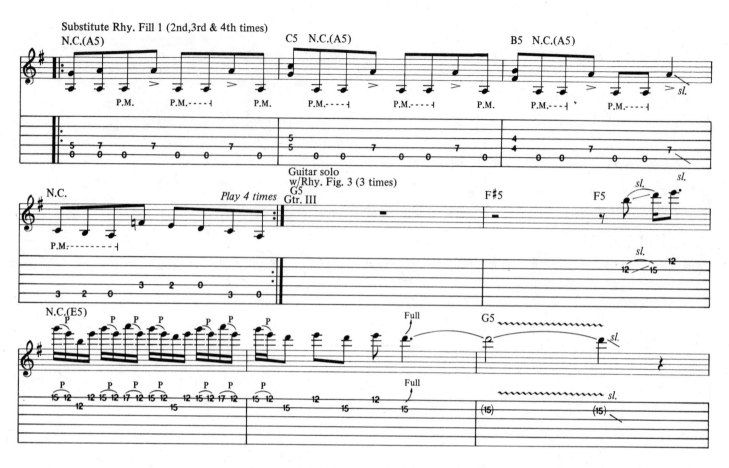

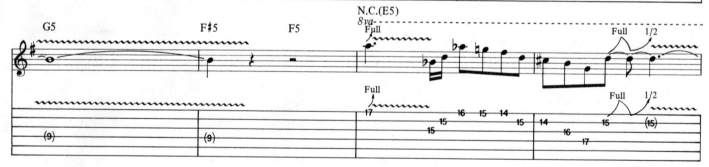

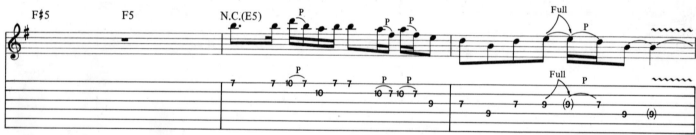

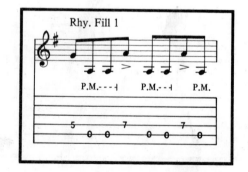

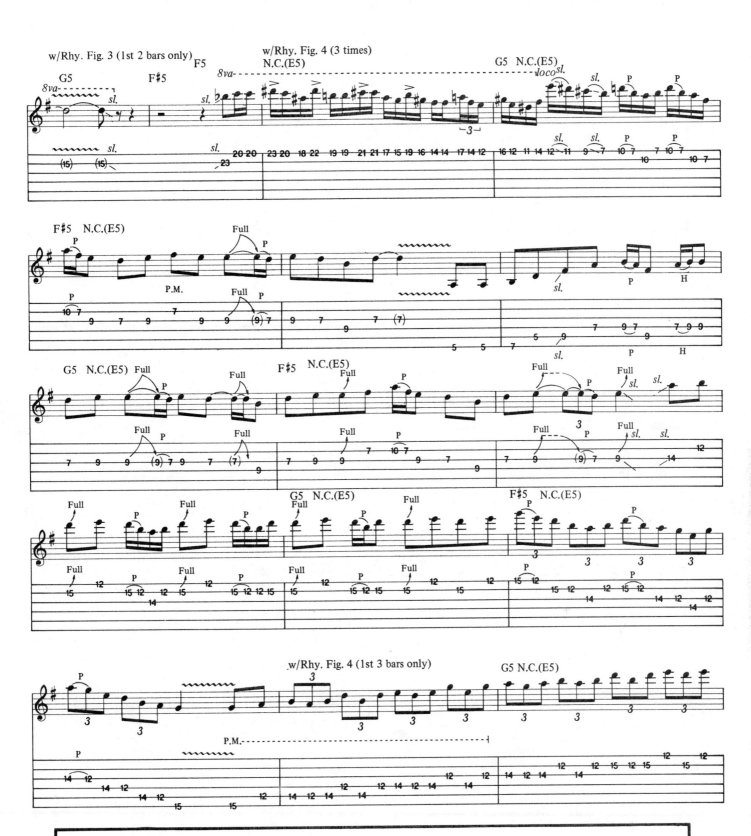

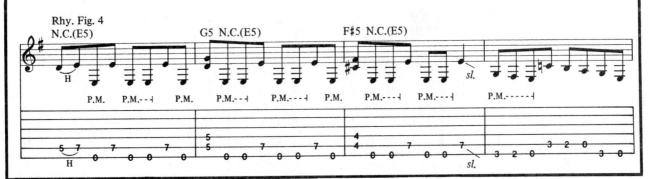

Additional Lyrics

2. There is no escape and that's for sure.
   This is the end we won't take anymore.
   Say goodbye to the world you live in.
   You've always been taking, but now you're giving. *(To Pre-chorus)*

3. Our brains are on fire with the feeling to kill.
   And it won't go away until our dreams are fulfilled,
   There is only one thing on our minds.
   Don't try running away 'cause you're the one we will find. *(To Pre-chorus)*

METAL MILITIA

**Words and Music by James Hetfield,
Lars Ulrich and Dave Mustaine**

w/Rhy. Fig. 2 (Gtrs. I & II)

N.C.

Eb5 Bb5 C5 G5 A5 Bb5

1'st, 2nd, 3rd Verses
w/Rhy. Fig. 2 (4 times)
N.C.

Eb5 Bb5 C5 G5 A5 Bb5

1. Thun - der and light - ning. The gods take re - venge.   Sense - less de - struc - tion.
2.3. *See additional lyrics*

N.C.

Eb5 Bb5 C5 G5 A5 Bb5

Vic - tims of fu - ry are cow - ard - ly now.   Run - ning for safe - ty.

N.C.

Eb5 Bb5 C5 G5 A5 Bb5

Stab - bing the har - lot to pay for her sins.   Leav - ing the vir - gin.

N.C.

Eb5 Bb5 C5 G5 A5 Bb5

Su - i - cide run - ning as if it were free.   Rip - ping and tear - ing.__

Pre-chorus
D5   C5   B5   A5(type 2) D5   C5   B5 C5

P.M.

Oh!__   Through the mist   and the mad - ness._____   We're try-ing to get the mes - sage to

3rd time to Coda II

(end Rhy. Fig. 3)

Chorus
Rhy. ⑤open
Fig. 3 A   C5 D5   ⑤open A   Eb5 D5 ⑤open A   C5 ⑤open A   Eb5 D5 C5

P.M.   P.M.   P.M.   P.M.

you.

Met - al mi -

w/Rhy. Fig. 3 (3 times) (3rd time 1st 3 bars only)

⑤open   ⑤open   ⑤open   *4th time to Coda I* ⑤open
A   C5 D5 A   Eb5 D5 A   C5 D5   A   Eb5 D5 C5

1.2.

li - tia!

Met - al mi -

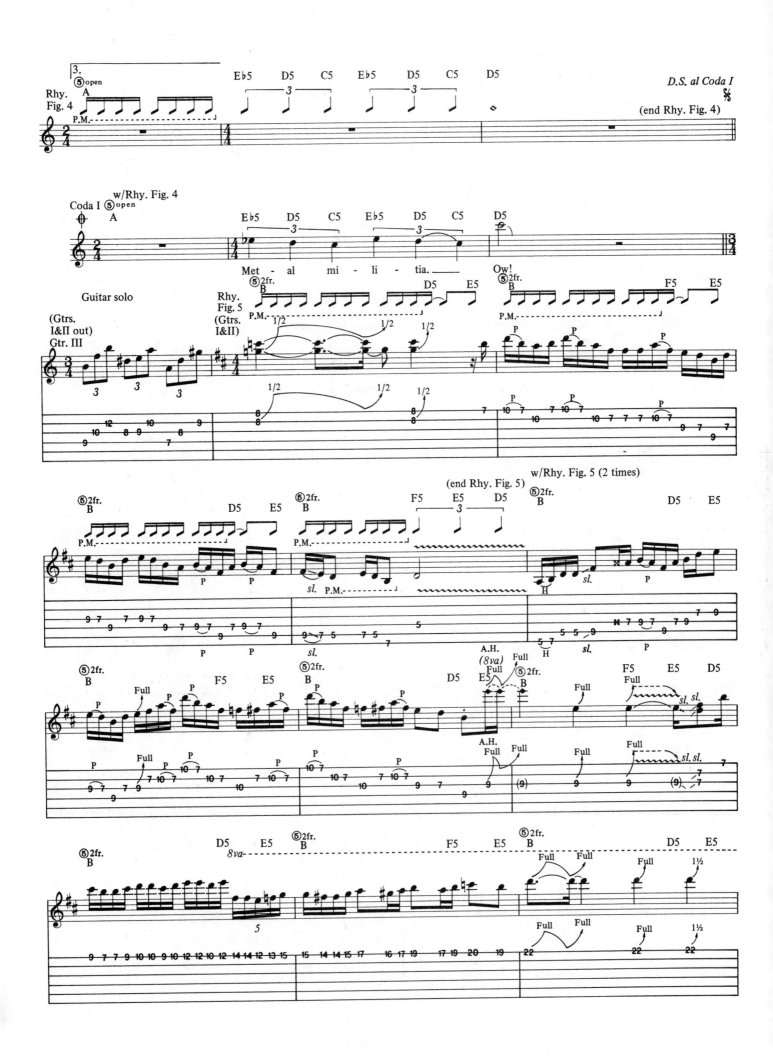

Additional Lyrics

2. Chained and shadowed to be left behind,
   Nine and one thousand.
   Metal militia for your sacrifice,
   Iron-clad soldiers.
   Join or be conquered, the low of the land.
   What will befall you?
   The metalization of your inner soul,
   Twisting and turning. *(To Pre-chorus)*

3. We are one as we all are the same,
   Fighting for one cause.
   Leather and metal are our uniforms,
   Protecting what we are.
   Joining together to take on the world
   With our heavy metal.
   Spreading the message to everyone here.
   Come let yourself go. *(To Pre-chorus)*

AM I EVIL?

Words and Music by Brian Tatler
and Sean Lindon Harris

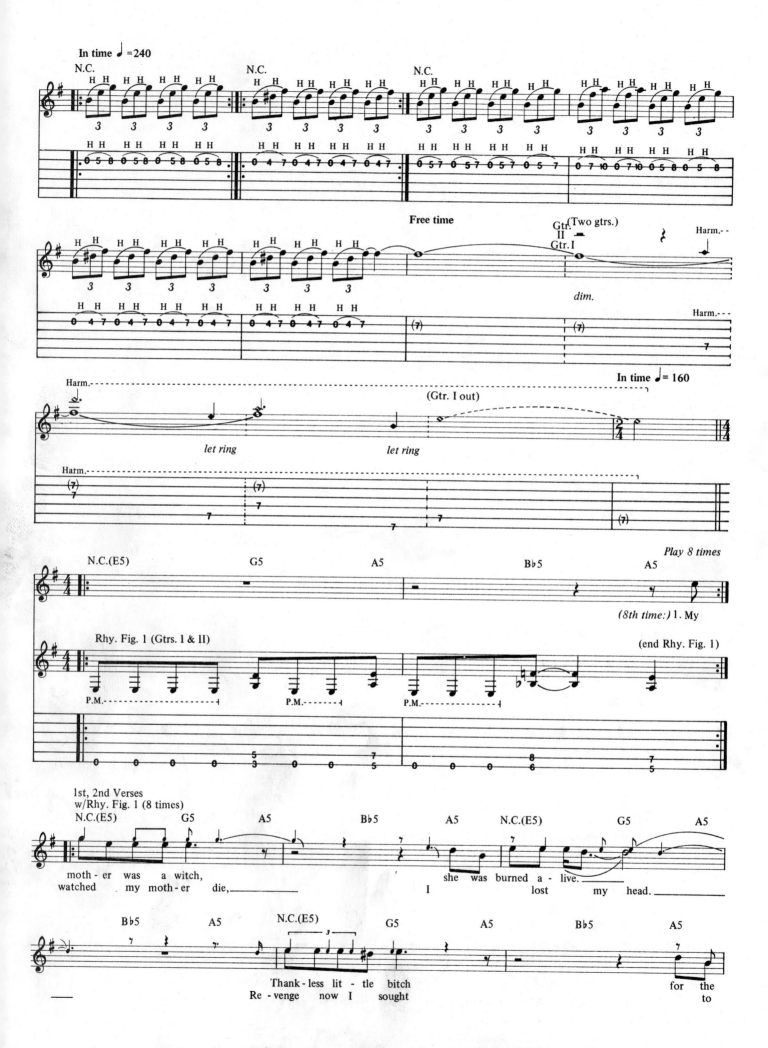

N.C.(E5) G5 A5 B♭5 A5 N.C.(E5) G5 A5
tears I cried.
break with my bread.
Take her down now,
Tak - in' no chan - ces,
B♭5 A5 N.C.(E5) G5 A5 B♭5 A5
don't want to see her face.
you come with me.
All
N.C.(E5) G5 A5 B♭5 A5 N.C.(E5) G5 A5
blis - tered and burnt,
I'll split you to the bone,
can't hide my dis - grace.
help set you free.
Pre-chorus
Rhy. Fig. 2
(end Rhy. Fig. 2)
⑥7fr. B D5 E5(type 2) F5(type 2)
P.M.
Twen - ty - sev - en, ev' - ry one was nice.
w/Rhy. Fig. 2 (3 times)
Got - ta see 'em, make 'em pay their price.
See their bod - ies out on
the ice.
Take my time.
Chorus I
w/Rhy. Fig. 1 (5 times)
Am I e - vil?
Yes, I am.
Am I e - vil?
I am man.
1.
Yes, I am.
2.
Rhy. Fig. 3
E5(type 2) D5 C5
2. As I
Yes, I am.
Gtr. II substitute Rhy. Fill 1
(2nd & 3rd times only)
w/Rhy. Fig. 1
(end Rhy. Fig. 3) N.C.(E5) G5 A5 B♭5 A5
w/Rhy. Fig. 3
E5(type 2) D5 C5
Play 3 times
Oh!

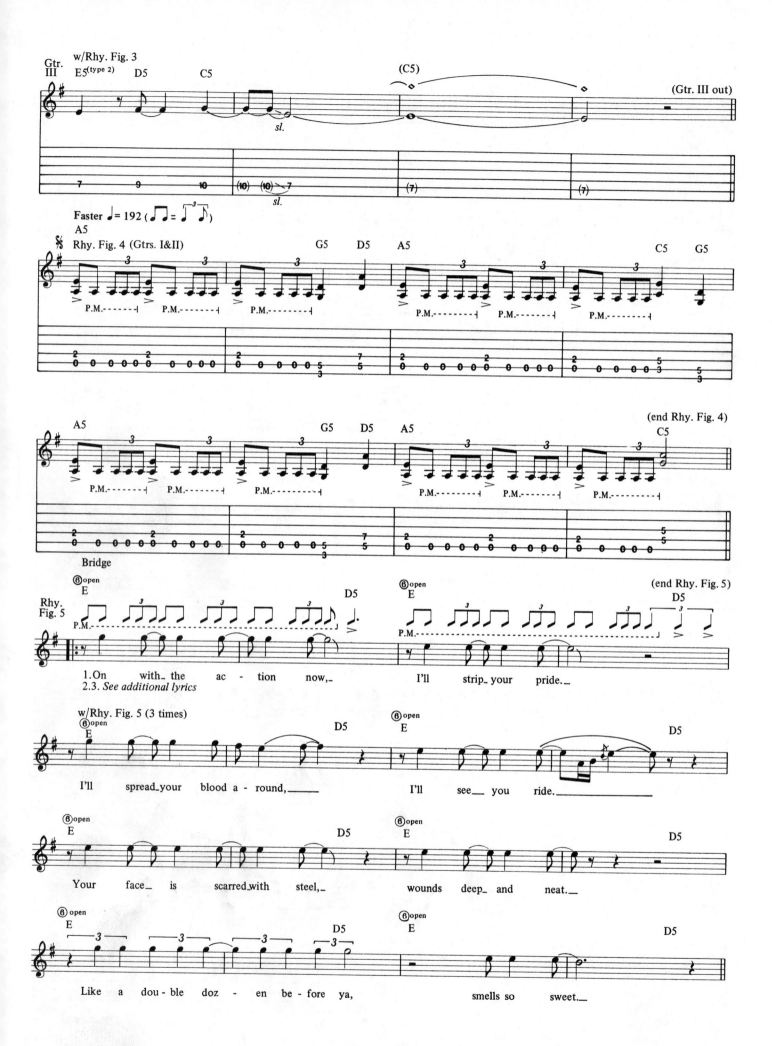

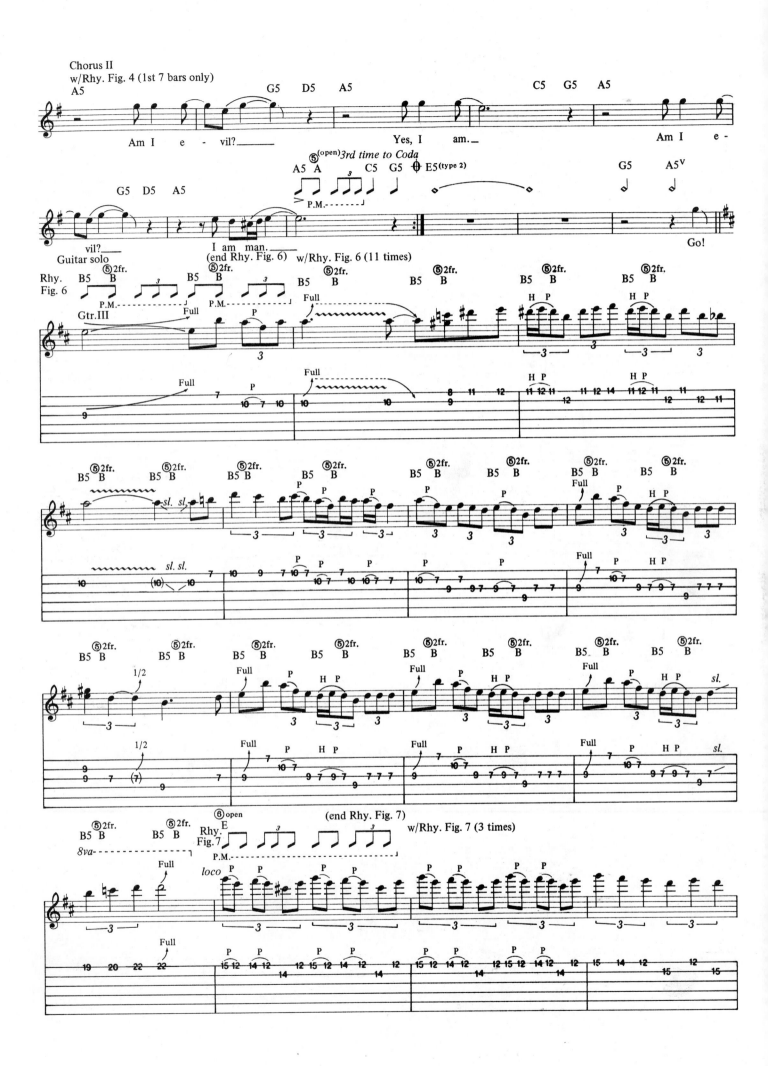

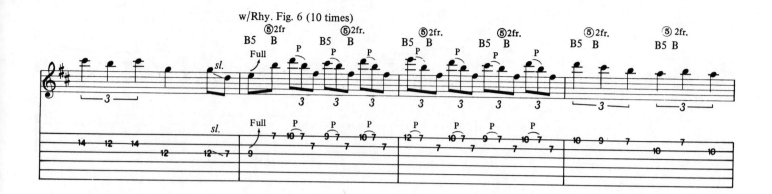

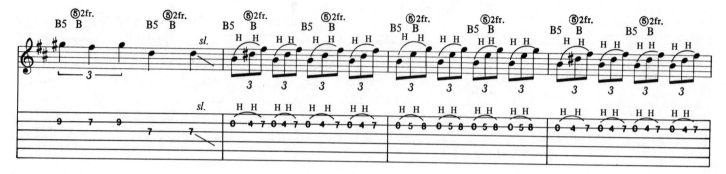

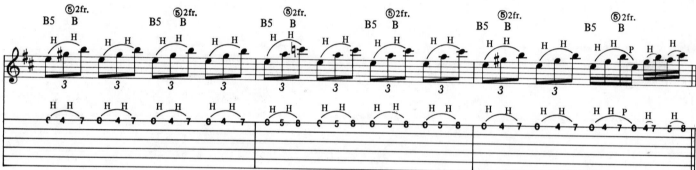

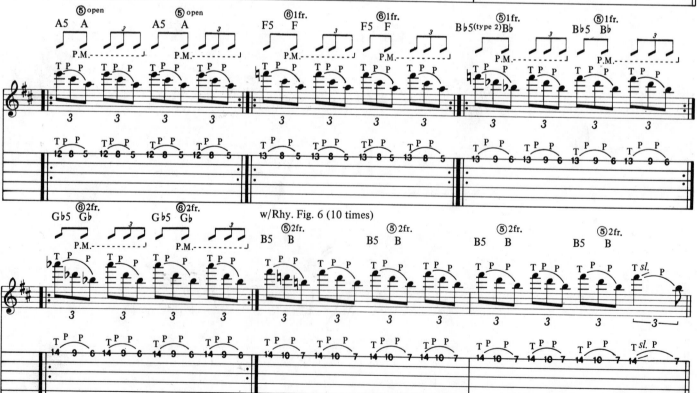

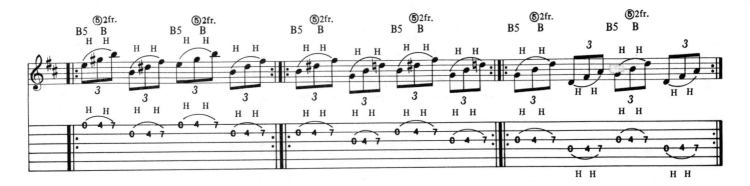

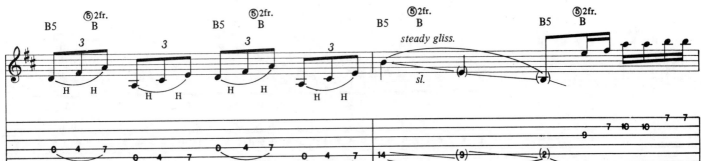

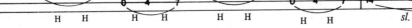

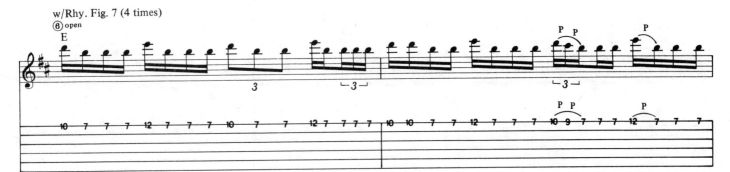

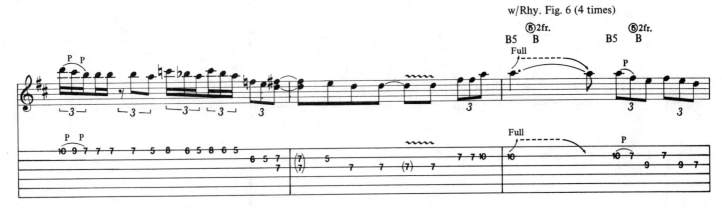

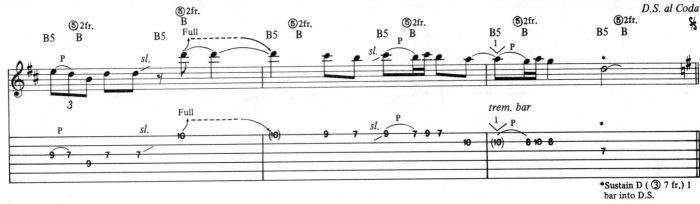

Additional Lyrics

2. I'll make my residence, I'll watch your fire.
   You can come with me, sweet desire.
   My face is long forgot, my face not my own.
   Sweet and timely whore, take me home. *(To Chorus II)*

3. My soul is longing for, await my heir,
   Sent to avenge my mother, sleep myself.
   My face is long forgot, my face not my own.
   Sweet and timely whore, take me home. *(To Chorus II)*

BLITZKRIEG

Words and Music by Ian Jones,
Brian Smith and James Sirotto

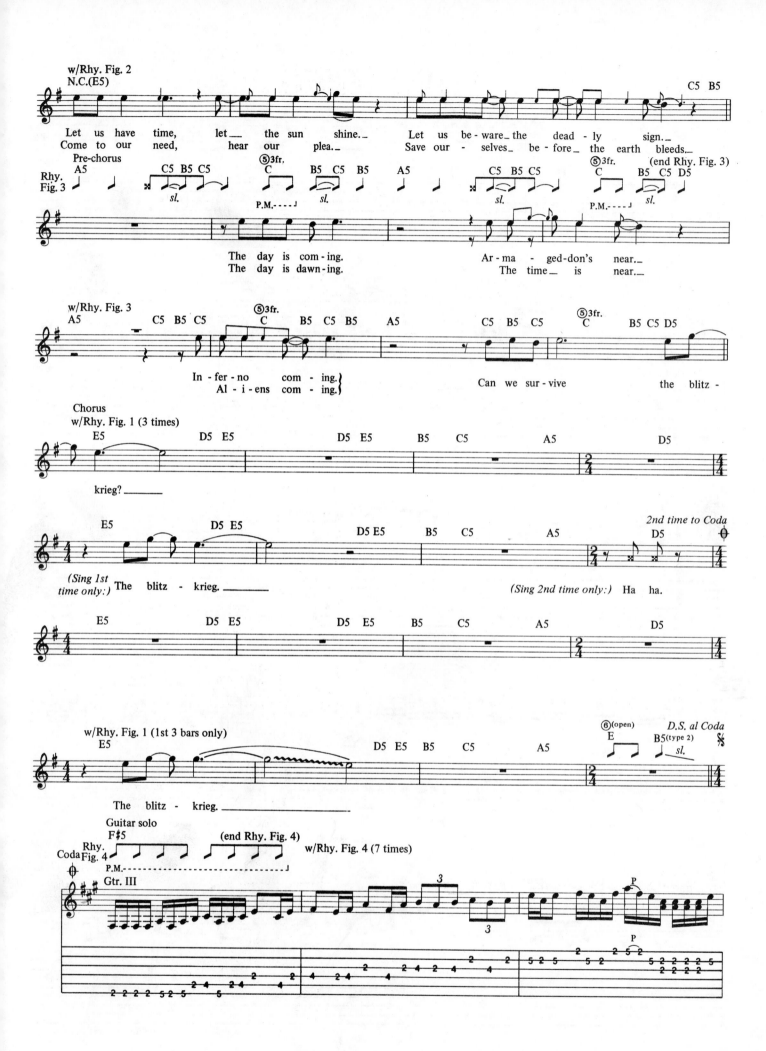

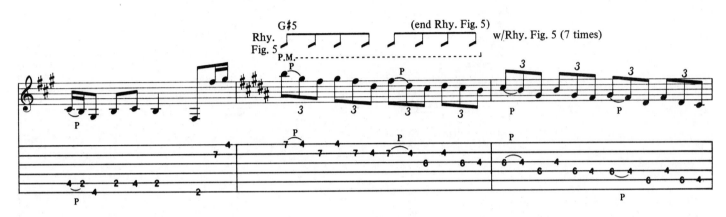

*Two gtrs. arr. for one (this bar only).

*Two gtrs. arr. for one (next 2 bars only).

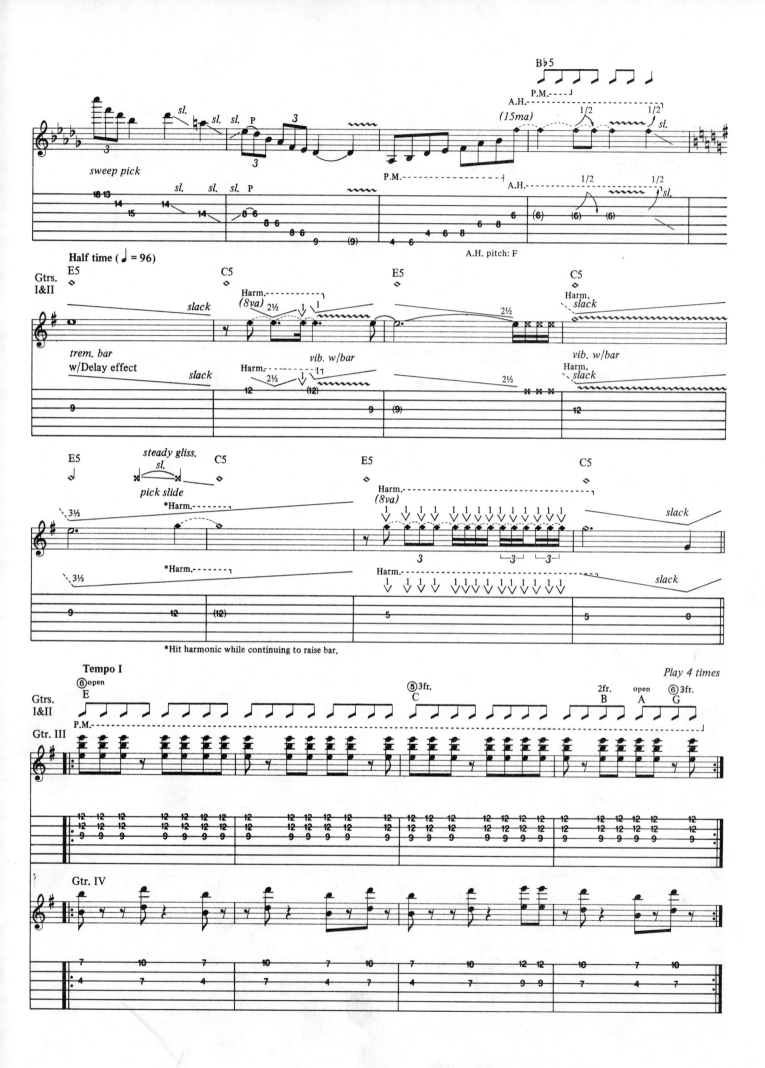

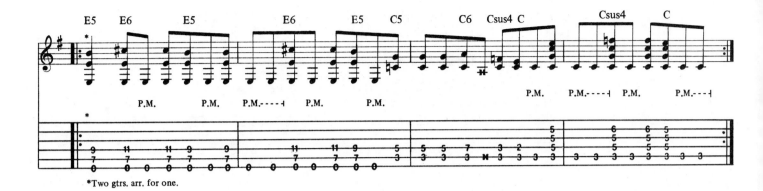

*Two gtrs. arr. for one.

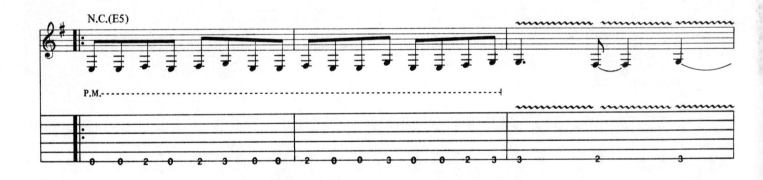

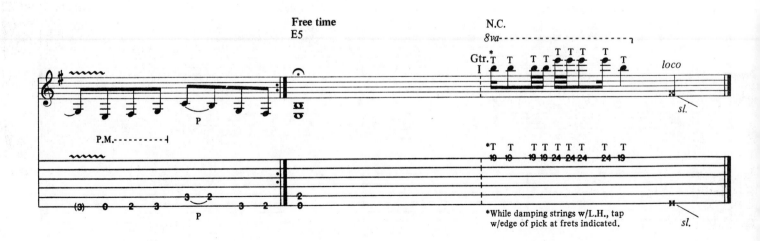

*While damping strings w/L.H., tap
w/edge of pick at frets indicated.

BUILD THE GUITAR LIBRARY
OF THE FUTURE WITH

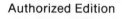
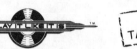

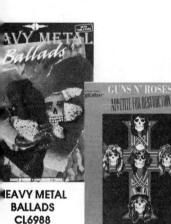
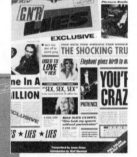
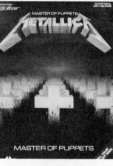
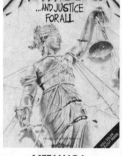
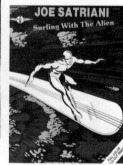
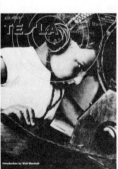
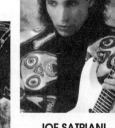
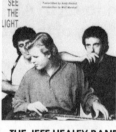

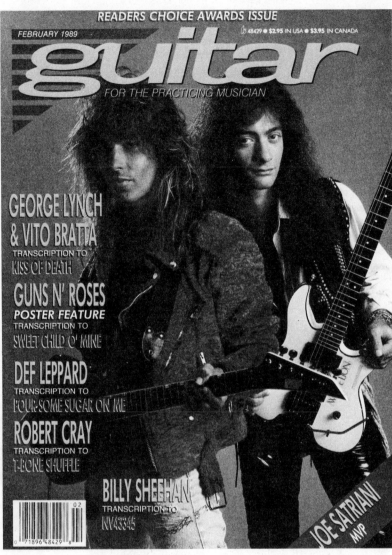